FAN PHENOMENA

SHERLOCK HOLMES

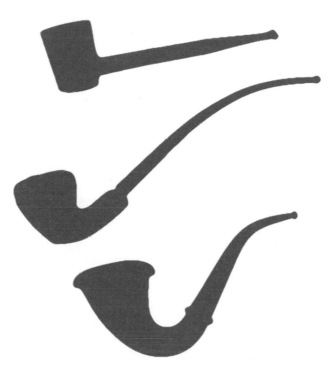

EDITED BY
TOM UE
AND JONATHAN CRANFIELD

Credits

First Published in the UK in 2014 by Intellect Books,
The Mill, Parnall Road, Fishponds, Bristol, BS16 3JG, UK

First Published in the USA in 2014 by Intellect Books,
The University of Chicago Press, 1427 E. 60th Street,
Chicago, IL 60637, USA

Copyright © 2014 Intellect Ltd

Editors: Tom Ue and Jonathan Cranfield

Series Editor and Design: Gabriel Solomons

Typesetting: Gabriel Solomons

Copy Editor: Emma Rhys

A Catalogue record for this book is available from
the British Library

Fan Phenomena Series
ISSN: 2051-4468
eISSN: 2051-4476

Fan Phenomena: Sherlock Holmes
ISBN: 978-1-78320-205-8
eISBN: 978-1-78320-273-7

Printed and bound by
Bell & Bain Limited, Glasgow

Contents

Fan Appeciation no.1
44—51
Anthony Horowitz:
Author of *The House of Silk*

5
Introduction
TOM UE AND JONATHAN CRANFIELD

8—27
Sherlock Holmes and Shakespeare
TOM UE

28—43
Holmes and the Snake Skin Suits:
Fighting for Survival on '50s Television
RUSSELL MERRITT

Fan Appeciation no.2
60—65
Ellie Ann Soderstrom:
Author of *Steampunk Holmes:
Legacy of the Nautilus*

52—59
Doyle or Death? An Investigation into the World of Pastiche
LUKE BENJAMEN KUHNS

Fan Appeciation no.3
80—89
The Team behind
*The Young Sherlock
Holmes Adventures*

66—79
Sherlock Holmes, Fan Culture and Fan Letters
JONATHAN CRANFIELD

90—99
Sherlock Holmes in the Twenty-second Century:
Rebranding Holmes for a Child Audience
NOEL BROWN

110—117
On Writing New Adventures on Audio: Into the Interstices of Canon
JONATHAN BARNES

118—123
The Creation of 'The Boy Sherlock Holmes'
SHANE PEACOCK

Fan Appeciation no.4
100—109
Scott Beatty:
Co author of
Sherlock Holmes: Year One

134—147
Getting Level with the King-Devil:
Moriarty, Modernity and Conspiracy
BENJAMIN POORE

148—151
Contributor Biographies

152
Image Credits

Fan Appeciation no.5
124—133
Robert Ryan:
Author of *Dead Man's Land*

Acknowledgements

Tom Ue thanks the Canadian Centennial Scholarship Fund; the Social Science and Humanities Research Council of Canada; and University College London.
Jonathan Cranfield thanks Jacquie and Leslie. We thank Gabriel Solomans, Emma Rhys, and our contributors for their hard work, and we gratefully acknowledge permission to reprint updated versions of the following material:

Tom Ue, *Sherlock Holmes and Shakespeare*. 2011 Cameron Hollyer Memorial Lecture (Toronto: Toronto Reference Library, 2012).
Tom Ue, 'Returning to Year One: A Conversation with Scott Beatty'. The Baker Street Journal: *An Irregular Quarterly of Sherlockiana* 62: 4 (2012), pp. 26–32.
Tom Ue, 'Holmes' Return: An Interview with Anthony Horowitz'. The Baker Street Journal: An Irregular Quarterly of Sherlockiana 62: 1 (2012), pp. 22–27.
Tom Ue, 'Holmes Steampunked: A Conversation with the Team behind The Young Sherlock Holmes Adventures.' The Baker Street Journal: An Irregular Quarterly of Sherlockiana 61: 3 (2011), pp. 23–31.
Shane Peacock, 'The Creation of The Boy Sherlock Holmes'. The Baker Street Journal: An Irregular Quarterly of Sherlockiana 58: 4 (2008), pp. 17–21.

Introduction
Tom Ue and Jonathan Cranfield

→ '... do what you like with him.'
(Arthur Conan Doyle)

When Arthur Conan Doyle gave the actor and playwright William Gillette free reign to interpret and to revise the character of Sherlock Holmes in any way that he saw fit, he spoke truer, perhaps, than he could have known. This collection attests to the popularity of the characters and fictional world that Conan Doyle created. Theodor Adorno's theorization of the 'culture industry' could have been written with Sherlock Holmes in mind: 'the more the system of "merchandizing" culture is expanded, the more it tends also to assimilate the 'serious' art of the past by adapting this art to the system's own requirements.' Yet, as Linda Hutcheon argues, an adaptation's adherence to the original should not be used as a barometer for measuring the work's worth: we can appreciate an adaptation more fully by reading it as a 'repetition but without replication' and, more specifically here, as a means for new generations of artists to engage in conversation with their literary predecessor. Hutcheon suggests that our appreciation for adaptations stems from the new aspects they bring to a text:

[An adaptation] is not a copy in any mode of reproduction, mechanical or otherwise. It is repetition but without replication, bringing together the comfort of ritual and recognition with the delight of surprise and novelty. *As adaptation*, it involves both memory and change, persistence and variation. (original emphasis).

The first decades of the twenty-first century have seen numerous incarnations of Holmes. Readers of this book will discover more about the Guy Ritchie films, distributed by Warner Brothers, the BBC's television production of *Sherlock* (Mark Gatiss and Steven Moffat, 2010-), the audio drama versions of Sherlock Holmes stories by Big Finish, alongside novels by Anthony Horowitz, Governor General's Literary Award (Children's Text)-finalist Shane Peacock and Robert Ryan. Their work explicitly references the 1950s radio productions by NBC which featured the likes of John Gielgud, Ralph Richardson and Orson Welles. The fictional fertility of the stories have inspired the work of graphic novelists Scott Beatty and Daniel Indro and the team behind *The Young Sherlock Holmes Adventures* (2010), Huw-J Davies, Owen Jollands and Jane Straw, two projects that provide backstories to the sleuth. While all of these projects retain some of the features with which we identify with Holmes, what is striking here is their sheer range: Ellie Ann Soderstrom discusses the publication of the iPad app *Steampunk Holmes: Legacy of the Nautilus* (Noble Beast, 2013). Tom Ue's chapter explores Conan Doyle and Holmes as fans of Shakespeare, and how they turn to his stories and characters in their projects. Russell Merritt tells the story of Holmes's migration from motion picture theatres to television; Luke Benjamen Kuhns provides a basic vocabulary for our thinking about Holmesian pastiches; Jonathan Cranfield examines fan letters directed to Holmes; and and Noel Brown finds *Sherlock Holmes in the 22nd Century* (Sandy Ross, STV, 1999-2001) both an updating of the stories into the far future and an ideological transformation of Conan Doyle's stories into didactic, educational lessons for school-age children. Jonathan Barnes and Shane Peacock offer critical reflections, respectively, on the teaching of Holmes and his recreation of the detective for Big Finish, and the creation of a past for the detective. Finally, Benjamin Poore looks at more contemporary adaptations of Holmes, particularly the BBC's *Sherlock*, as projects that channel manifestations of post-9/11 conspiracy-anxiety.

Hutcheon offers the trope of memes to foreground the evolution and mutation of adaptations to fit new times and different places. 'We retell–,' she writes, 'and show again and interact anew with – stories over and over; in the process, they change with each repetition, and yet they are recognizably the same. What they are not is necessarily inferior or second-rate – or they would not have survived. Temporal precedence does not mean anything more than temporal priority.' By following Conan Doyle's injunction to 'do what you will', the figure of Holmes has been constantly refreshed and renewed, adapted, like memes, to new cultural moments without a diminishment of his appeal for new audiences. The injunction in the new age of fanfiction, social media and e-commerce is not simply to consume passively but instead to be a creative participant. The figure of Holmes, laced with nostalgia, has proven to be the most enduring model for the ways in which this new model can operate. ●

GO FURTHER

Books

Memories and Adventures
Arthur Conan Doyle
(Cambridge: CUP, 2012)

A Theory of Adaptation
Linda Hutcheon
(New York: Routledge-Taylor, 2006)

The Culture Industry
Theodor Adorno
(London: Routledge-Taylor, 2003)

'IT HAS LONG BEEN AN AXIOM OF MINE THAT THE LITTLE THINGS ARE INFINITELY THE MOST IMPORTANT.'

SHERLOCK HOLMES
'A CASE OF IDENTITY'

Chapter
1

Sherlock Holmes and Shakespeare

Tom Ue

→ Early on in *A Study in Scarlet* (2003; Vol. I), Watson deftly sums up his first impression of Holmes's knowledge of literature with the word 'Nil', though, Watson allows, '[h]e appears to know every detail of every horror perpetuated in the century.'[1] As Watson learns more about Holmes, many of his early impressions, like this, are put into question. Holmes's 'ignorance *was* as remarkable as his knowledge' (emphasis added). He may not know the extremely influential nineteenth-century essayist, historian, novelist and social and political commentator Thomas Carlyle and his writing, yet Holmes's reading ranges widely from Petrarch's sonnets to Honoré de Balzac's and George Meredith's fiction, from miracle plays to Henry David Thoreau's journal, and from early English charters and Shakespeare's plays to criminal news, agony columns and the *Newgate Calendar*. Let us not forget 'Humpty Dumpty'. Holmes's reading provides a lens through which we can gain a whole new appreciation for both his stories and Conan Doyle's aesthetics, and as Tanya Agathocleous puts it,

> Holmes' scientific outlook [...] is importantly allied with artistic experience – his tortured appreciation of the violin and his 'immense' knowledge of sensational literature prepare him for his crime-solving as well as, if not better than, his knowledge of either chemistry or the law.

> Conan Doyle returns to Shakespeare time and again. In *The Hound of the Baskervilles* (2003; Vol. I), for example, the cabdriver, who carried the man dogging Sir Henry and Dr Mortimer, told the surprised Holmes and Watson that the man had given his name. 'Oh, he mentioned his name, did he? That was imprudent. What was the name that he mentioned?,' asked Holmes, as he 'cast a swift glance of triumph' at Watson. The cabman's response – that the man had claimed to be 'Mr. Sherlock Holmes' – moved the real Holmes into confessing defeat: 'A touch, Watson – an undeniable touch!' In a seemingly unrelated scene, in *The Valley of Fear* (Vol. II), Holmes interrupts Watson's periodic statement in which he identifies Professor Moriarty as a 'famous scientific criminal, as famous among crooks as [...] he is unknown to the public'. Although Watson's annoyed response at being interrupted for the second time that morning is not narrated to us on this occasion, it nevertheless leads Holmes to cry: 'A touch! A distinct touch! [...] You are developing a certain unexpected vein of pawky humour, Watson, against which I must learn to call myself.'
>
> These two scenes share in common – besides Holmes's being proven wrong – a gesture to Hamlet and Laertes's fencing match in Act V Scene II of *Hamlet*, and a synthesis of Osric's identification of Hamlet's successful hit as 'A hit, a very palpable hit' and Laertes's of another as 'A touch, a touch, I do confess'. If, in the play, both Hamlet and Laertes fight a losing battle – Hamlet, because he little suspects that Laertes will fight with a sword that is not blunted and that he will coat it with poison; and Laertes, because he is used by Claudius – the sword touch, from Holmes's lips, is indicative of his mock and not his actual (much less mortal) defeat, as the appearance of both allusions in the early chapters of both mysteries would suggest. Holmes exaggerates his despondency and his defeat, and we are meant to respond to his comic resignation with a smile. Conan Doyle's parodies of the Danish prince here reveal a sophisticated command of his source material and the skill with which he rewrites and adapts Shakespeare freely and for different ends. The Victorians knew their Shakespeare. Conan Doyle experienced Shakespeare in a variety of formats including, quite possibly, H. M. Paget and Walter Paget's 1890 booklet *Shakespeare Pictures* and H. M.'s title page for *The Graphic: An Illus-*

Sherlock Holmes and Shakespeare
Tom Ue

trated *Weekly Newspaper* on 19 November 1892, which showed Ellen Terry as Cordelia and Henry Irving as Lear.[2] In what follows, I will explore some of the numerous ways in which Shakespeare's writing affected Conan Doyle in his creation and writing of Sherlock Holmes and his stories. My aims are to put Conan Doyle's reading of Shakespeare at the heart of his own writing, while giving a glimpse of the literary and social debates at the turn of the nineteenth century with which he was actively engaged, and to show Conan Doyle and Holmes themselves as fans in their own right. This chapter is divided into three parts. The first examines Conan Doyle's views about the authorship question by analysing some of his nonfiction and his poetry. The second argues that drama informs both the narrative structure of Conan Doyle's short stories and Holmes's methods. The third examines how Conan Doyle rewrites Shakespeare through close readings of 'The Boscombe Valley Mystery' (Vol. I) and 'The Missing Three-Quarter'.

Conan Doyle and Shakespeare
Conan Doyle writes, in a letter to Charlotte Drummond, on 12 April 1888:

> Poor old Shakespeare! I fear it is all up with him. Alas and alas for the good burghers of Stratford! Alas too and alas for the globe trotting Yankees who have come from the other end of the world to gaze upon the habitation of the man who did not write the plays! What a topsey-turveydom it is! There were many reasons before this to think that Bacon was the true author, but if the Cryptogram on being tested proves to be true it is simply conclusive. (original emphasis)

The Cryptogram refers to a system devised by Ignatius Donnelly, a Baconian whose thousand-page magnum opus *The Great Cryptogram: Francis Bacon's Cipher in the So-Called Shakespeare Plays* (1888) 'scores already familiar points about the illiteracy of Shakespeare and the profound learning (especially legal learning) displayed in the plays', notes Schoenbaum. More interesting is the sheer number of works that Donnelly attributes to Bacon:

> This busy scribbler penned Montaigne's *Essays*, Burton's *Anatomy*, the numerous plays of Shakespeare apocrypha, a bit of Peele, and the whole Marlowe corpus. [...] [A]fter all, Donnelly calculates, if Bacon took time out from his public life and private studies to dash off a play every fortnight from 1581 to 1611 (why not?) he would have written "seven hundred and eighty plays!"'

The Da Vinci Code (Dan Brown, 2004) pales in comparison with Donnelly's cipher, which he finds embedded in Parts 1 and 2 of *Henry IV*:

> 'A long, continuous narrative, running through many pages, detailing historical

events in a perfectly symmetrical, rhetorical, grammatical manner.' Such a narrative, 'always growing out of the same numbers, employed in the same way, and counting from the same, or similar starting-points cannot be otherwise than a prearranged arithmetical cipher.'

As Schoenbaum has revealed, *The Great Cryptogram* and its imperfect and, by no means, impartial mathematician were received by 'an ungrateful world [...] with disbelief, indifference, or laughter,' yet '[t]hat Donnelly's methods were loose and vulnerable only spurred on others to find the key that would break the code'. What is striking about these attempts to understand Shakespeare through cipher is a commitment to and a knowledge of Shakespeare the man and his work. The personal involvement and emotional investment of these late Victorians seem to suggest that in discovering the truth about Shakespeare, they will learn more about themselves, and that, on a more personal level, Shakespeare *speaks* to them.

Conan Doyle returns to the authorship question in his introduction, as chairman of the Authors' Club, to Sidney Lee, the prominent Shakespearian and editor of the *Dictionary of National Biography*, on 31 October 1910.[3] He expresses his wish that Lee 'will not brush aside the Baconian hypothesis as unworthy of refutation, but will deal with it, however straitly'. Conan Doyle admits his own ambivalence when it comes to the authorship question:

I suppose it is the result of a perverse habit of always seeing the other side of a question, but I have found that an aggressive Shakespearian statement has usually inclined me to Bacon while an interview with a rabid Baconian has invariably brought me back to orthodoxy.

He proceeds to give an anecdote of a visitor armed with a facsimile of Ben Jonson's dedication in the folio:

He explains to me that if I took a root number and counted the letters backwards and then looked at them upside down – that was the general impression conveyed to my mind – I would always come on the number 1623 which was the year of publication. Since the year was printed on [the folio] and was never in dispute I confess I could not understand why the information should be conveyed in so roundabout a fashion. But when my instructor proceeded to point out that by some other juggle I could always get 1910, which proved that Jonson had foreseen that that was the year on which the mystery would be solved, I began to feel my faith in Shakespeare considerably fortified.

While it is likely that additional juggling of numbers would bring them to 2011, and

Sherlock Holmes and Shakespeare
Tom Ue

possibly even to some combination of today's date, Conan Doyle admits that 'we must at least give [this gentleman] credit for the courage of his convictions' and, more importantly, that no matter who the writer of Shakespeare's works is, he remains 'the most wonder[ous] [sic] creative machine that the world has ever seen, the widest in its range of sympathy, the broadest in its emotions, the most dainty in its fancy, [and] the most felicitous in its choice of expression'. The more mature Conan Doyle, then, privileges Shakespeare's work over the man.

Conan Doyle refers to Shakespeare in two poems: 'H.M.S. "Foudroyant"' and 'Shakespeare's Expostulation'. He returns to the authorship question in the latter, a dramatic monologue in blank verse – the metre Shakespeare used most often – that was collected in his 1911 volume *Songs of the Road*. Made restless in his grave by 'crazy wrights' who insist that Bacon had authored Shakespeare's plays, the unnamed monologist of 'Expostulation' spells out and responds to the argument that Shakespeare could not have known all that he knows to write his plays. The speaker reasons that although he was denied learning in colleges, 'Yet may a hungry brain still find its food / Wherever books may lie or men may be.' He addresses the claim that Shakespeare was a college fellow:

If I be suspect, in that I was not
A fellow of a college, how, I pray,
Will Jonson pass, or Marlowe, or the rest,
Whose measured verse treads with as proud a gait
As that which was my own? Whence did they suck
This honey that they stored? Can you recite
The vantages which each of these has had
And I had not? Or is the argument
That my Lord Verulam [Bacon] hath written all,
And covers in his wide-embracing self
The stolen fame of twenty smaller men?

The recite-ability of Shakespeare's work is telling: most of us can recite a line or two from *Hamlet* without having read it. The centrality of recitation cannot be overstated: in the nineteenth-century, memorization and performance in school plays – often Shakespeare's – are central to the education system and poetry was generally meant to be read aloud. However, familiarity with Shakespeare's writing does not *prove* that it is written by the man himself, and this crux is made more prominent as the poem progresses. The speaker cites the 'want of learning' reflected in his writing as evidence that he is the author: 'Have I not traced / A seaboard to Bohemia, and made / The cannons roar a whole wide century / Before the first was forged?' And yet, his awareness of these factual errors need not suggest a lack of learning since he could very well have made them on purpose in an attempt to pass them as Shakespeare's. If these errors are made accidentally, they do not prove that Bacon did not make them. He says, of Bacon's now-discovered poems, 'You may read his verse, / And judge if mine be better or be worse: / Read and pronounce! The meed of praise is thine; / But still let his be his and mine be mine.' The speaker appeals to Jonson's epitaph and argues that their contemporaries 'must have smiled to see the marbled fraud' if indeed he is one, and he makes a final plea: 'My brow shall speak when Shakespeare's voice is dumb, / And be his warrant in an age to come.' If the speaker's argument seems suspect since images of his forehead prove nothing, since he never identifies himself as Shakespeare, and since he does not claim Shakespeare's voice as his own in the lines quoted above, the monologue as a whole only raises questions about what it seeks to prove: we are uncertain who the speaker is. Indeed, the poem's very title is precariously unclear about whether it is Shakespeare protesting or a protest made on his behalf.

Sherlock Holmes and drama

As in Conan Doyle's poem, the Sherlock Holmes canon is a site of negotiations. Holmes's home, *The Strand Magazine*, is a middle-class-oriented monthly of immense popularity from its inaugural issue in January 1891 to its final in March 1950. Priced at sixpence – significantly less than most established journals and more than the penny papers, as noted by Wiltse – it is distinct from the yellow-backed novels for which Watson has developed such aversion in 'The Boscombe Valley Mystery'. As Wiltse suggests, thematically, Conan Doyle's stories reflect this middle ground for literature: they occupy a liminal position that defines itself against

> both the 'low' culture, [composed of] true crime narratives so popular throughout the nineteenth century, and [...] the 'fantastic' detective tales that Holmes scorns when Watson tries to compare his own newly minted professional specialty to the activities of Poe's Dupin and Gaboriau's Lecoq.

Holmes tells Watson:

> If we could fly out of that window hand in hand, hover over this great city, gently remove the roofs, and peep in at the queer things which are going on, the strange coincidences, the plannings, the cross-purposes, the wonderful chains of events, working through generation, and leading to the most *outré* results, it would make all fiction with its conventionalities and foreseen conclusions most stale and unprofitable.

Here, Holmes draws on the first of Hamlet's soliloquies in the passage. In Act I Scene II, he rails – 'O God, O God, / How weary, stale, flat, and unprofitable / Seem to me all the uses of this world!' – against his mother Gertrude's and, more generally, woman's in-

Sherlock Holmes and Shakespeare
Tom Ue

fidelity. Ed Wiltse connects Holmes to Hamlet. '[T]he final allusion to Hamlet,' for Wiltse

> that other alienated, hyper-ratiocinative bachelor, that other man who knew too much, at once reinforces Holmes's disconnection from the normative social 'conventionalities' he is purported to police, and reminds us that unlike Hamlet, Holmes gets away with his mad behaviors.[4]

What Hamlet sees as immoral in Denmark – the severity of which is shown to us by the sheer panic of the sentinels at the start of the play – and, more importantly, what he tries to rectify, Holmes sees as the limits of literary realism. Watson largely agrees with Holmes's desire for realism,[5] as we may infer from his dismissal of a yellow-backed novel in 'The Boscombe Valley Mystery'. His criticism betrays his preoccupation with story:

> The puny plot of the story was so thin, however, when compared to the deep mystery through which we were groping, and I found my attention wander so continually from the fiction to the fact, that I at last flung it across the room and gave myself up entirely to a consideration of the events of the day.

Holmes criticizes Watson's writing time and again. In response to Watson's write-up of *A Study in Scarlet*, for example, Holmes tells him in *The Sign of Four* (Vol. I):

> Some facts should be suppressed, or, at least, a just sense of proportion should be observed in treating them. The only point in the case which deserved mention was the curious analytical reasoning from effects to causes, by which I succeed in unravelling it.

It is only when Holmes comes to write his own stories in 'The Adventure of the Blanched Soldier' and in 'The Adventure of the Lion's Mane' (Vol. II), that he recognizes the need to covet the reader's interest, and that 'had [Watson] but been with [him] [...] he might have made [much] of so wonderful a happening and of [Holmes's] eventual triumph against every difficulty!' ('The Adventure of the Lion's Mane'). Watson is understandably hurt by Holmes's vocal and predominantly unflattering criticism, as he protests in *The Sign of Four*:

> I was annoyed at this criticism of a work [*A Study in Scarlet*] which had been specifically designed to please him. I confess, too, that I was irritated by the egotism which seemed to demand that every line of my pamphlet should be devoted to his own special doings. More than once during the years that I had lived with him in Baker Street I had observed that a small vanity underlay my companion's quiet and didactic manner.

Within the Sherlock Holmes stories, drama is a central theme. In 'The Wisteria Lodge' (Vol. II), Holmes expresses his doubt that Watson could narrate it 'in that compact form which is dear to [his] heart': 'It covers two continents, concerns two groups of mysterious persons, and is further complicated by the highly respectable presence of our friend, Scott Eccles.' Despite Holmes's concern over the limits of the short-story form, Conan Doyle repeatedly shows us that it is hospitable to multiple viewpoints, and genre conventions, just as *The Strand* is to many kinds of writing. At the end of 'The Norwood Builder' (Vol. II), for example, Holmes specifically tells Watson what to narrate when he asks Jonas Oldacre: 'By the way, what was it you put into the wood-pile besides your old trousers? A dead dog, or rabbits, or what? [...] If ever you write an account, Watson, you can make rabbits serve your turn.' Watson's decision to narrate this request, rather than simply to honour it, effectively juxtaposes and dramatizes the two characters' views within the framework of a short story. If drama informs the narration of the Holmes stories, so too does it play a pivotal role in his methods and, by that, I refer not only to his demonstrated acting chops: his credits range from playing a non-conformist clergyman to a rakish young workman, and from feigning a nervous attack to an opium hobby.[6] In 'The Norwood Builder', Holmes draws on idioms of drama to create for Watson and Lestrade a scenario that satisfies all of the circumstances that the seemingly-guilty John McFarlane described:

> The older man is showing documents which are of evident value. A passing tramp sees them through the window, the blind of which is only half down. Exit the solicitor. Enter the tramp! He seizes a stick, which he observes there, kills Oldacre, and departs after burning the body.

Both the stage directions and the short emphatic statements with which Holmes describes his case gesture towards his stage-inspired thinking, and this becomes more apparent in his theatre metaphor in 'The Second Stain' (Vol. II): 'Come, friend Watson, the curtain rings up for the last act.'

Holmes, the dramatist, and Watson and Lestrade, his audience, and we, as the readers, are brought together in a metatheatrical scene in 'The Six Napoleons' (Vol. II), after he produces the famous black pearl of the Borgias,

> Lestrade and I sat silent for a moment, and then, with a spontaneous impulse, we both broke out clapping, as at the well-wrought crisis of a play. A flush of colour sprang to Holmes's pale cheeks, and he bowed to us like the master dramatist who receives the homage of his audience. It was at such moments that for an instant he ceased to be a reasoning machine, and betrayed his human love for admiration and applause.

Sherlock Holmes and Shakespeare
Tom Ue

Holmes is a dramatist through and through. In *The Valley of Fear* (Vol. II), for example, he describes Barker's and Mrs Douglas's rehearsed account as being 'badly stage-managed', and momentarily, he explains why he refuses – as he frequently does – to 'waste words or disclose [his] thoughts while a case is actually under consideration' ('The Blanched Soldier'):

> Watson insists that I am the dramatist in real life [...] Some touch of the artist wells up within me, and calls insistently for a well-staged performance. Surely our profession, Mr. Mac, would be a drab and sordid one if we did not sometimes set the scene so as to glorify our results. The blunt accusation, the brutal tap upon the shoulder – what can one make of such a *dénouement*? But the quick inference, the subtle trap, the clever forecast of coming events, the triumphant vindication of bold theories – are these not the pride and the justification of our life's work? At the present moment you thrill with the glamour of the situation and the anticipation of the hunt. Where would be that thrill if I had been as definite as a timetable? (*The Valley of Fear*)

Of course, it is infinitely more thrilling for us, who trust Holmes and who are reading his stories in comfy armchairs by fireplaces – real or artificial – and who are reading these stories as accounts told in retrospect, and for Holmes, who knows what he is doing, than it is for his frequently under-informed allies, particularly when they face the un-alluring prospects of bitter vigils and mortal dangers. Holmes is quite honest when he confesses to Lord Cantlemere in 'The Mazarin Stone' (Vol. II), 'I can never resist a dramatic situation.'

Conan Doyle and revision
Conan Doyle's own astuteness as reader and adaptor manifests clearly in 'The Boscombe Valley Mystery' and 'The Missing Three-Quarter', both of which nod to his close friend George Meredith's writing. In 'The Boscombe Valley', Charles McCarthy is found murdered, and all evidence incriminates his son James: he is seen by a game-keeper to be following his father and carrying a gun under his arm; a lodge-keeper's daughter witnesses a violent quarrel between the two and James 'rais[ing] up his hand as if to strike his father'; James is the first to discover his dying father, and he appears before the lodge-keeper 'without either his gun or his hat, and his right hand and [his] sleeve [...] stained with fresh blood'; and James refuses, despite three requests from the coroner, to explain the reasons behind the quarrel. However, the McCarthys' landlord John Turner's daughter Alice believes James sufficiently to retain Lestrade to prove his innocence; Lestrade, of course, calls on Holmes and Watson. Holmes's preface to his narrative, to Watson and to us as readers, of James and Alice's romance – 'Ah, thereby hangs a rather painful tale' – gestures to one or more speaker(s) from three possible plays: in *As*

You Like It, Jaques tells the Duke Senior about his encounter with Touchstone; in *Othello*, the clown asks the musician not to perform; and in *The Taming of the Shrew*, Grumio describes, to Curtis and to us, the early trials of Petruccio's and Katherine's marriage. The possible comic and tragic outcomes associated with this allusion echo, I believe, the embedded narrative's very ambivalence. The prosaic Holmes sums up James and Alice's romance in a single rhetorical question:

> This fellow is madly, insanely, in love with her, but some two years ago, when he was only a lad, and before he really knew her, for she had been away five years at a boarding-school, what does the idiot do but get into the clutches of a barmaid in Bristol and marry her at a registry office?

James's desire to conceal this marriage prevents him from confessing to Alice, who reciprocates his affections; to his insatiable father, upon whom he is dependent financially; and to the coroner when he asks James why he quarrelled with his father. However, as Holmes reveals to Watson:

> Good has come out of evil […] for the barmaid, finding from the papers that he is in serious trouble and likely to be hanged, has thrown him over utterly and has written to him to say that she has a husband already in the Bermuda Dockyard, so there is no tie between them.

After telling this story and revealing the mystery's two cruxes – that McCarthy had no appointment with his son, and that he gave the Australian cry 'Cooee!' before he knows of his son's return – Holmes tells Watson: 'And now let us talk about George Meredith, if you please, and we shall leave all minor matters until to-morrow.' Holmes is not diverting attention away from the case when he turns to Meredith, and Conan Doyle's name-dropping here is not incidental. He wrote prolifically on Meredith, and in an article on Robert Louis Stevenson in January 1890 for the *National Review*, he cites Meredith as a central influence for late-Victorian writers:

> Meredith was made to be imitated. His mission is not so much to tell stories himself, as to initiate a completely new method in the art of fiction, to infuse fresh spirit into a branch of literature which was in much need of regeneration. His impatient and audacious genius has refused to be fettered by conventionalities. He has turned away from the beaten and well-trod track, and has cleared a path for himself through thorny and doubtful ways. Such a power would have worked in vain were there not younger men who were ready to follow closely in his steps, to hold what he has gained and to strike off from it to right and to left.

Sherlock Holmes and Shakespeare
Tom Ue

Conan Doyle belonged to this generation, and 'The Boscombe Valley' borrows heavily from Meredith's first full-length novel *The Ordeal of Richard Feverel: A History of
a Father and Son* (1859), which alludes to a number of Shakespeare's plays, but most
prominently to *The Tempest*.[7] If Prospero's and Miranda's intimacy is deepened owing to
their exile in an island, this relationship is recreated in that of Sir Austin and Richard in
Meredith's novel. The narrator explains why Richard is not permitted to attend school:

> Sir Austin considered that the schools were corrupt, and maintained that young lads
> might by parental vigilance be kept pretty secure from the Serpent until Eve sided
> with him: a period that might be deferred […] He had a system of education for his
> son.

Sir Austin's segregation of and his attempt to provide a safe space for Richard's
physical, emotional and intellectual growth continuously backfire as he repeatedly sub-
verts his father's control, and finally meets and falls in love with Lucy Desborough, a
local farmer's niece. His system succeeds in more ways than one – it continues to exert
pressure on Richard in his every decision – and Martha A. Turner rightly attributes the
system's tragic consequences to Sir Austin:

> Sir Austin would say that his system does not manipulate nature but rather allows for
> his son to grow up in harmony with it. Yet in actuality the Baronet intervenes repeat-
> edly. He polices his son's activities and exerts authority when he disapproves – most
> notably when he seeks to destroy Richard's 'natural' love for Lucy.

Richard marries Lucy against his father's wishes, though this marriage is cut short
when Richard separates from his wife in hopes of eventually securing his father's approval. Eventually, Richard betrays his wife by having an affair, and becomes so ashamed
that he continues their separation. During this time, Lucy discovers that she is pregnant
with Richard's child and, with the birth of a son, Sir Austin begins to relent. Upon discovering that his prolonged abandonment of Lucy had nearly caused her to be seduced,
Richard challenges Lucy's seducer to a duel in France, and we learn, from a letter from a
Lady Blandish, that Richard received a gunshot wound, an event that catalyses his wife
Lucy's fever and death, which, in turn, made him wear 'the expression in the eyes of blind
men' as he, in the novel's final words, 'striv[es] to image her on his brain'. Meredith's use
of a narrative frame to mediate this event, which might have served as the novel's climax, makes more apparent the ironic distance between how Richard views the duel and
how Meredith and the reader view it. This narrative strategy mitigates the duel's heroic
promise and for Gladys W. Ekeberg, regardless of its outcome, 'Richard's character and
future happiness have been marred by the tragic ordeal he has passed through'. However, the singularized ordeal of the novel's title can well gesture towards this very duel,

an event that 'acts as a test, or severely tests character or endurance' ('Ordeal' [def. #2]). As Poston notes, Meredith's choices do not mitigate the novel's tragic resolution, which leaves open the possibility of Richard following Sir Austin's footsteps in his own parenthood, or Meredith's awareness of the tragic potential to be found in *The Tempest*. Conan Doyle gestures to both Shakespeare's play and Meredith's work through the external pressures that James's and Alice's parents place on them – James's father, like Prospero, tries to make him marry Alice for their social and financial betterment – and, more specifically, to Meredith's novel through James's infidelity to the constant Alice as a consequence of his youth and ignorance.

Conan Doyle returns to Meredith in his later story 'The Missing Three-Quarter', in which the missing Godfrey Staunton is attached to and marries his landlady's daughter, despite his being heir to a nobleman who would disinherit him because of this marriage The similarities of the two works are most apparent when, by the story's conclusion, we find the young widower, like the blinded Richard, 'so dazed that he could not be made to understand that [Holmes and Watson] were anything but doctors who had been sent to his assistance'. However, just as Meredith revises Shakespeare, Conan Doyle actively rewrites Meredith's from a tragedy wherein Richard is tried to the point that he is unable to articulate his and Lucy's joint sufferings to mysteries that conclude more ambiguously. In the case of 'The Boscombe Valley', Watson reveals that, with the death of Turner, 'there is every prospect that the son and daughter may come to live happily together in ignorance of the black cloud which rests upon their past' and in the case of 'The Missing Three-Quarter', Holmes and Watson find Godfrey's 'frame [...] racked by his sobs'. The inclusion of these romances, and Conan Doyle's ending of both mysteries by returning to them, spur us to read with greater attention. The marriage plot has a knack of operating as social and formal resolutions in Victorian writing and I would argue that Conan Doyle and Watson purposefully deny us of the certainty and of the imminence of James and Alice's marriage in preference for an ending that is as ambivalent as Shakespeare's for *The Tempest*, and present, through Godfrey's marriage, one that is as tragic as Meredith's. Conan Doyle's take on romance in these two stories, I believe, is synecdoche of a larger conflict in his treatment of the past and its bearing on the present and the future. In his brilliant chapter on Holmes, Barry McCrea argues persuasively that the marriage plot is substituted by – what the title of his book suggests – a company of strangers:

> In the Holmes stories, generative possibility is not to be found in the untangled family line or in marriage but in the infertile encounters of unrelated individuals that they produce. As 221B replaces the structuring center of the family plot, Holmes and Watson's partnership replaces the narrative trope of marriage.

Sherlock Holmes and Shakespeare
Tom Ue

The fact that James and Alice are ignorant of the circumstances behind McCarthy's murder neither mitigates nor obviates the burden of the past on their future, a burden that is composed of the mutual aversion of Turner and McCarthy, their aversion for the other's children – as evidenced, for instance, by Turner's identification of James as 'cursed stock' and McCarthy's 'urging his son to marry [Turner's] daughter as if she were a slut from off the streets' – or the possible return of the bigamist barmaid, particularly in light of the number of stories in the canon that involve blackmail. Meanwhile, 'the house of grief' from which Holmes and Watson depart by the end of 'The Missing Three-Quarter' leaves open the possibility that Godfrey could channel his grief in more productive directions and that he could protest more actively against his uncle. Conan Doyle's incorporation of Shakespeare and Meredith does not suggest a divorce from Conan Doyle's contemporary issues, but rather, I think, provides a new and more complex engagement with them. For Ed Wiltse, Foucauldian readings of the Holmes stories – readings that mark how 'science, medicine and the law collude to 'discipline and punish transgression at every level of society' – overlook what he rightly identifies as Holmes's 'alternative lifestyle': 'Drug addicted, intermittently employed, gynephobic, and powerfully bonded with Watson, Holmes is obliquely positioned with respect to the crucial, even definitive, bourgeois doctrine of productivity in myriad ways.' McCrea goes further when he argues – and I believe the open-ended conclusions of both 'The Boscombe Valley' and 'The Missing Three-Quarter' and the antithesis that they pose to the restoration of genealogical and social order would support this – that Holmes is an agent not of order but of change:

> The families turn to Holmes to reassure and help them, but what he offers – despite all of the showy rhetoric about atavism and the like – is a means of understanding the world through an antigenealogical, queer system based on plotting rather than natural succession, on adjacency rather than heredity.

If, as Miss Burnet asks, in 'The Wisteria Lodge', 'What does the Law of England care for the rivers of blood shed years ago in San Pedro, or for the shipload of treasure which this man had stolen?', Conan Doyle's short stories also ask his readers a version of the same question in relation to events much closer to home. In 'The Speckled Band' (Vol. I), for example, Helen Stoner appears to Holmes and Watson 'in a pitiable state of agitation, her face all drawn and gray, with restless, frightened eyes, like those of some hunted animal'. Aged before her time, her behaviour and circumstance, as McCrea says, betray that she knows much more than she lets on,

> Helen Stoner rushes as fast as the train and dog cart will carry her to consult Holmes at 221B Baker Street, shaking with the knowledge that her stepfather will imminently try to murder her as he has already done to her sister.

Dr Roylott's tyranny manifests in his treatment of both members of his household and his neighbours, as Helen reveals:

Instead of making friends and exchanging visits with our neighbours, who had at first been overjoyed to see a Roylott of Stoke Moran back in the old family seat, he shut himself up in his house and seldom came out save to indulge in ferocious quarrels with whoever might cross his path.

In sum, the ill-used Helen tells Holmes and Watson, and us, as readers,

You can imagine from what I say that my poor sister Julia and I had no great pleasure in our lives. No servant would stay with us, and for a long time we did all the work of the house. She was but thirty at the time of her death, and yet her hair had already begun to whiten, even as mine has.

Similarly, in 'Black Peter' (Vol. II), the detective Stanley Hopkins describes the bully that was the late Captain Peter Carey: he 'was an intermittent drunkard' who 'has been known to drive his wife and daughter out of doors in the middle of the night and flog them through the park until the whole village outside the gates was aroused by their screams'. Hopkins's account is corroborated by Watson, who observes that the eyes of Carey's widow 'told of the years of hardship and ill-usage which she had endured', and that her daughter's 'eyes look defiantly at [them] as she told [them] that she was glad that her father was dead, and that she blessed the hand which had struck him down'. Dr Roylott and Captain Carey are known publicly as tyrants and irresponsible patriarchal figures, and yet no one has made an effort to help these women. Indeed, without Holmes, Watson and Conan Doyle, their stories would have been obscured.

Holmes has read *Hamlet* though he is not the Danish prince. By seeing Holmes as a custodian of order and panopticism, we might overlook, what Watson has identified as, his 'kindliness' and Conan Doyle's and his character's preoccupations, as is in keeping with late Victorian thought, with ethics. In 'A Case of Identity' (Vol. I), for instance, Holmes tells the dishonest though not, strictly speaking, criminal James Windibank: 'The law cannot, as you say, touch you [...] yet there never was a man who deserved punishment more. If the young lady has a brother or a friend, he ought to lay a whip across your shoulders.' In more ways than one, Holmes is both a brother and a friend to those in need of help. In 'The Engineer's Thumb' (Vol. I), Watson calls attention to the difference between experiencing and reading about a mystery:

The story has, I believe, been told more than once in the newspapers, but, like all such narratives, its effect is much less striking when set forth *en bloc* in a single

Sherlock Holmes and Shakespeare
Tom Ue

half-column of print than when the facts slowly evolve before your own eyes, and the mystery clears gradually away as each new discovery furnishes a step which leads on to the complete truth.

I believe that Watson's description of the process of reading as one of a detective as he tries to solve a case provides a useful analogy for our thinking of Shakespeare's and Conan Doyle's writing. The two writers' razor-sharp dialogue and their persistent desire, as Conan Doyle has put it in his address to the Authors' Club, to see the other side of a question enable them to deconstruct the social structures that they seem to reaffirm at the levels of language and narrative. Both Holmes's fervency and his vocalized ambitions to define himself against the governmental intelligence and the official police force emblemized, respectively, by his brother Mycroft and by Scotland Yard underscore his individuality and his independence. Holmes's dexterity as a character offers a basic analogy for the reader's very own experience as he or she unpacks the work before him or her and if, as Adrian Poole says, 'We can all see ourselves in Shakespeare', so too can we all see ourselves in Sherlock Holmes. ●

Notes
1. Holmes returns to these early impressions when he tells Watson in 'The Five Orange Pips' (2003; Vol. I): 'If I remember rightly, you on one occasion, in the early days of our friendship, defined my limits in a very precise fashion.' All references to the Holmes stories are to the Barnes and Noble version and will be cited by volume.
2. Copies of both were found in the Arthur Conan Doyle Collection Lancelyn Green Bequest, Portsmouth City Council. While it is unverifiable if they belonged to Conan Doyle or Green, the former is familiar with the Pagets and their work.
3. In a letter to Mary Doyle in September 1910, Conan Doyle refers to this address as a lecture to be given on 29 October 1910.
4. Watson also draws on *Hamlet* to describe Holmes in 'The Reigate Puzzle' (2003; Vol. I), 'I have usually found that there was method in his madness.'
5. See 'The Mazarin Stone', in which Conan Doyle uses a third-person narrator to bring together both Holmes's and Watson's experience, and to dramatize, effectively, the story for the audience. We are as surprised as Count Sylvius and Sam Merton, when Holmes – in a move evocative of Polonius – uses his bedroom's second door, which leads behind a curtain, to hide behind it and to listen in on them. We do well to recognize Polonius's potential complicity in Claudius's usurpation or, at the very least, his unquestioning support and encouragement of that king.
6. Holmes disguises himself on numerous occasions: he adopts the appearance and demeanour of 'The Dying Detective' to mislead Mrs Hudson, Watson and Culverton Smith; in 'The Illustrious Client' (2003; Vol. II), Watson confesses that he 'had suspicions at times that [Holmes] was really finding himself [after an injury] faster than he pretended

even to [him]'; and in 'The Mazarin Stone', Holmes posed as an out-of-work workman and an old woman. Holmes confesses to Count Sylvius in that story: 'Old Baron Dowson said the night before he was hanged that in my case what the law had gained the stage had lost.'

7. All references, unless indicated otherwise, are to the Charles Scribner's Sons edition of *The Ordeal of Richard Feverel* which uses the 1896 text.

Acknowledgements

This paper was first given on 30 April 2011 at the Toronto Reference Library and first published as the 2011 Cameron Hollyer Memorial Lecture. It is dedicated to Philip Horne, and I am much indebted to him for his incisive reading. An abridged version was presented in the lecture series of the 2011 University College London Department of English Language and Literature Summer School. I thank my audience members and students for their incisive feedback. For all kinds of help, I thank Rosemary Ashton, Christine Bolus-Reichert, Jason Boyd, Fiona-Jane Brown, Cliff Goldfarb, Michael Gunton, John James, Roger Johnson, Jon Lellenberg, Fiona Luck, Barry McCrea, Dayna Nuhn, Peggy Perdue, Brian Pugh, Steven Rothman, and Daniel Stashower. My thanks go to the staff of the following: the Arthur Conan Doyle Collection, Toronto Public Library; The Arthur Conan Doyle Collection Lancelyn Green Bequest, Portsmouth City Council; the British Library; Senate House Library, University of London; and University College London Library. I would like to thank the Friends of the Arthur Conan Doyle Collection at the Toronto Public Library, the Social Science and Humanities Research Council of Canada, Canadian Centennial Scholarship Fund, and University College London.

Sherlock Holmes and Shakespeare
Tom Ue

~~~~~~~~~~

GO FURTHER

Books

Urban Realism and the Cosmopolitan Imagination in the Nineteenth Century: Visible City, Invisible World
Tanya Agathocleous
(Cambridge: CUP, 2011)

In the Company of Strangers: Family and Narrative in Dickens, Conan Doyle, Joyce, and Proust
Barry McCrea
(New York: Columbia University Press, 2011)

Arthur Conan Doyle: A Life in Letters
Arthur Conan Doyle
Jon Lellenberg, Daniel Stashower and Charles Foley (eds) (London: Harper P-Harper Collins Publishers, 2007)

The Man Who Created Sherlock Holmes: The Life and Times of Sir Arthur Conan Doyle
Andrew Lycett
(New York: Free Press, 2007)

Shakespeare's Lives
S. Schoenbaum
(New York: Barnes & Noble, 2006)

The Oxford Shakespeare: The Complete Works
William Shakespeare
John Jowett, William Montgomery, Gary Taylor, and Stanley Wells (eds) (Oxford: OUP, 2005; 2nd edn)

The Da Vinci Code: Special Illustrated Edition
Dan Brown
(New York: Doubleday-Random House Inc., 2004)

The Complete Sherlock Holmes, Volumes I and II
Arthur Conan Doyle
Kyle Freeman (ed.) (New York: Barnes and Noble Classics, 2003)

Mechanism and the Novel: Science in the Narrative Process
Martha A. Turner
(Cambridge: CUP, 1993)

Meredith: The Critical Heritage
George Meredith
Ioan Williams (ed.) (London: Routledge & Kegan Paul, 1971)

The Ordeal of Richard Feverel: A History of a Father and Son
George Meredith
Frank W. Chandler (ed.) (New York: Charles Scribner's Sons, 1917)

Shakespeare Pictures
H. M. Paget and Walter Paget
(London: Ernest Nister, 1890)

Extracts/Essays/Articles

'Falstaff's Belly, Bertie's Kilt, Rosalind's Legs: Shakespeare and the Victorian Prince'
Adrian Poole
In Peter Holland (ed.). *Shakespeare and Comedy* [Special issue of *Shakespeare Survey*]. 56 (2003) [Online], pp. 126–36, http://dx.doi.org/10.1017/CCOL0521827272.010.

'"So Constant an Expectation": Sherlock Holmes and Seriality'
Ed Wiltse
In Miriam Marty Clark (ed.). *The Short Story* [Special issue of *Narrative*]. 6: 2 (1998) [Online], pp. 105–22, http://www.jstor.org/stable/20107142.

'Dramatic Reference and Structure in *The Ordeal of Richard Feverel*'
Lawrence Poston, III
In *Studies in English Literature, 1500–1900: Nineteenth Century*. 6: 4 (1966) [Online], pp. 743–52, http://www.jstor.org/stable/449367.

'Mr Stevenson's Methods on Fiction'
Arthur Conan Doyle
In *National Review* (January 1890), p. xiv. [Repr. as 'Sir Arthur Conan Doyle on Meredith's "audacious genius"'. In Ioan Williams (ed.). *Meredith: The Critical Heritage* (London: Routledge & Kegan Paul, 1971), pp. 330–31].

Sherlock Holmes and Shakespeare
Tom Ue

'*The Ordeal of Richard Feverel* as Tragedy'
Gladys W. Ekeberg
In *College English*. 7: 7 (1946) [Online], pp. 387–93, http://www.jstor.org/stable/370639.

'Shakespeare's Expostulation'
Arthur Conan Doyle
In *The Poems of Arthur Conan Doyle* (London: John Murray, 1922), pp. 148–50.

'H.M.S. "Foudroyant"'
Arthur Conan Doyle
In *The Poems of Arthur Conan Doyle* (London: John Murray, 1922), pp. 41–42.

'[Speech, introducing Mr. Sidney Lee at the Authors Club dinner, London.]'
Arthur Conan Doyle, 1910. MS. Arthur Conan Doyle Collection, Toronto Public Library, Toronto.

'Revival of Shakespeare's *King Lear* at the Lyceum Drawn by H. M. Paget'
H. M. Paget
In *The Graphic: An Illustrated Weekly Newspaper*. XLVI (1892), p. 1.

Online

'Ordeal'. *Oxford English Dictionary Online*, September 2013.

'MY NAME IS
SHERLOCK HOLMES.
IT IS MY BUSINESS
TO KNOW WHAT OTHER
PEOPLE DON'T KNOW.'

'THE BLUE CARBUNCLE'

Chapter 2

Holmes and the Snake Skin Suits: Fighting for Survival on '50s Television

Russell Merritt

→ It is a tale madmen used to tell in the King Cole Bar, under a gigantic cartoon mural; a story for territory salesmen at the all-night delis in L.A. You could have read about it in *Billboard* or *Sponsor*, but not in *The Baker Street Journal*. In academic talk, it will lose its essential fragrance, sound a little sterile, turn into a bland little report about suits... unfamiliar middle men, advertizing executives, Hollywood players, and long-forgotten fights over feature films on television.

Fig. 1: *Sherlock Holmes on a 1950s TV Screen*

But listen. Odds are you have never seen a Basil Rathbone-Nigel Bruce Sherlock Holmes feature in a movie theatre. Almost certainly you never saw one as a double feature with a cartoon and newsreel. Instead, you discovered those films on television or, if you are under a certain age, on a digital screen where you likely streamed it. This is the way we encounter classic Hollywood films today, on TV screens and monitors where they have been revived since the early-1950s, and where their current reputations as cultural icons have been created. This is where the Universal Sherlock Holmes movies, like *The Wizard of Oz*, *It's A Wonderful Life*, or virtually any B-film noir prized today, were rehabilitated. It is where they emerged from the lukewarm reception critics gave them on their original release and found their abiding audiences among viewers brought up on late-night shows and daily matinees.

How Sherlock Holmes migrated from motion pictures to television has seldom been told, and for good reason. Today, when films move seamlessly from theatres to home screens, the transition seems automatic and unremarkable. But there was nothing inevitable about it in the early 1950s. Watching Sherlock Holmes movies on TV was made possible only by a series of cut-throat battles and shrewd calculations made over a short but remarkably eventful period of months. And when the films eventually emerged on television, the response ranged from delight to derision that passed into contempt.

Part of the mockery stemmed from the debased conditions under which the films were broadcast, conditions that today beggar the imagination. For a generation that had only seen movies projected in movie theatres [the one place you *could* see features, pre-TV], the new screen resembled a grotesque parody of a show place, where movies from a different era were strangely resurrected as contorted ghosts of their original 35mm selves.

The pictures were so snowy, small, and unstable that a viewer could hardly see what was happening. Scenes were brutally cut or condensed to make room for local commercials. Today, we are still familiar with commercial breaks. But not the slicing up of films to fit into hour-long time slots, nor with black-and-white images that wriggled and waved with interference patterns, or lost all depth when pasted onto ultra low-resolution screens. "How do you snip out 30% of a carefully made product and have it make sense?" the writer in a 1950 trade journal asked. His solution: "First, eliminate all dark scenes that won't show up on a TV tube, and then all the long shots in which distant objects get lost."[1] How to enlarge an image on a family TV set that could measure as little as 12" diagonally? Buy a specially designed magnifying glass that could be fitted in front of the screen.

Holmes and the Snake Skin Suits:
Fighting for Survival on '50s Television
Russell Merritt

And yet, particularly for those who had never seen 1930s and war-time films, they could be mesmerizing. A lost world had opened up, and it is a tribute to many of those films, including the Rathbone-Bruce series, that their pull could be so strong they survived even these conditions. And of special importance to Sherlockians, it was through this deeply flawed medium that the last and most famous of the Sherlock Holmes feature film series was kept alive.

The series debuted over KTTV in Los Angeles on 2 May 1954: as best we can tell, the first time any Sherlock Holmes feature film was televised anywhere in the United States. Here is the advertisement in the *Los Angeles Times* that provided the details. As Holmes might have said, there are several points not entirely devoid of interest.

Tonight's title, as the ad indicates, is *Sherlock Holmes and the Secret Weapon* - the second film in the original series. It is being broadcast not in the off hours customarily given to old films, but in prime time on a Sunday night, in the spring of that fateful year 1954. It is also being broadcast over an independent station, not a network affiliate, sponsored by "Your Nearest Pontiac Dealer," - a consortium of local dealers - but not by the national giant that owned the Pontiac brand, General Motors. And finally there is the Universal logo - significant because it is nowhere to be found, either in this ad, on any televised print, or in any promotional material.

All this points to a turning point in film exhibition, a curious mix of the old and new, with a studio still shy about acknowledging its involvement in the telecast of its own product, and an old movie still being shown by a local independent station when networks wanted nothing to do with movies. And yet there are quiet innovations: a feature being offered on prime-time, underwritten entirely by a single sponsor in a top broadcast market. We are not just at the start of an important Sherlockian revival. The ad also doubles as a snapshot of a pivotal point in the rapidly changing relationship between film studios and a looming monster medium.

1954. The famous freeze in the relations between Hollywood and the broadcast industry was in the midst of a great thaw, and the ongoing battle over whether to reissue the studios' vintage A-list movies on television was coming to a head. And though Universal's Sherlock Holmes series was emphatically a B-list series, it played a curious and crucial role as a wedge in that ongoing drama.

By the mid-50s there was, of course, nothing novel in re-running old films on TV. From virtually the start of commercial television, stations were notorious for filling their schedules with cheaply-made westerns, crime films, serials, discarded British imports, and cartoons from poverty-row studios. Even major studios - notably Universal, Paramount, and Twentieth Century-Fox - were surreptitiously putting many of their B-pictures, serials, and cartoons on the market. Nor was there anything new about showing quality films on television. As early as 1950, David O. Selznick's *Nothing Sacred* (1937) with Carole Lombard and Fredric March had run on New York's WNBT and *A Star is Born* (1937) on WPIX; during the same year Ford's *Stagecoach* (1939), Hitchcock's *Foreign Correspondent* (1940), and Lubitsch's *To Be or Not To Be* (1942) were syndicated as part of a package of features produced by Walter Wanger and Alexander Korda.

But these broadcasts were all under-the-counter, one-time only arrangements - covert operations where, to disguise their involvement, the major studios created sales through dummy companies, third parties and specially created studio subsidiaries whereby they could secretly engineer repurchase agreements In virtually every case, the contracts required that studio identifications and logos be removed from all prints before they reached the air.[2] The idea was to take advantage of the windfall profits made possible with one-off TV rentals without offending their theatre chains and, in particular, independent exhibitors who saw in the rise of television the principal cause for the decline of theatre attendance. Despite the ongoing process of divorcing themselves from their theatres, mandated by the famous 1947 Supreme Court decree, the majors were still eager to maintain the goodwill of independents and the most powerful exhibitors who were capable of boycotting studio product.

Universal was testing the water with their Holmes films - going further than any studio had before in defying the theatres by openly selling TV rights to the most prestigious and arguably most marketable '40s series in their catalog. With no theatres of their own to worry about, Universal was less vulnerable to reprisals than other majors, and the studio was gambling that the TV rentals would earn enough money to offset resentment from their peers. To limit the risk, Universal confined their sales to the Sherlock Holmes series, and as a precautionary measure hacked the company logo and other studio tags off their prints in the prescribed manner. Further still, they discreetly limited their series to selected markets - Los Angeles [KTTV], Tijuana [the bi-lingual XETV], Cincinnati [WCPO], Fresno, CA [KJEO], plus a few others. But within the trade itself, they made no secret of the sales. Trade journals reported them as Universal deals, while the company placated their critics reassuring them that while they were authorizing these licenses, the Sherlock Holmes broadcasts were "in no way indicative that Universal-International [Universal's successor company] will reverse its ban on releasing the U-I backlog of theatrical features to TV."[3] Though only two films in the series had been officially re-issued in theatres, Universal-International thought the series showed promise in a medium that was already exploiting lesser detective series like *The Falcon, Boston Blackie, Mr. Wong, Bulldog Drummond, The Shadow,* and *Philo Vance.* Of particular interest to U-I was the oldest and most prominent of the low-price pilot fish: the twenty Charlie Chan features from the 1930s that had been flooding local stations for over a year.

This was likely motive enough to resurrect Holmes. Then, too, networks had crime and detective series of their own. Further still, U-I likely considered the Rathbone-

Holmes and the Snake Skin Suits:
Fighting for Survival on '50s Television
Russell Merritt

Fig. 3: Holmes makes his Chicago debut on DuMont network affiliate WGN-TV. Chicago Tribune, 2 November 1954

Bruce films the logical bridge between Universal's long list of fillers that had already been snuck on TV, and their most valuable pre-1947 properties. The studio would not be willing to trade their prized assets - their famous '30s horror films, their Deanna Durbin musicals, and prestige pictures like *Shadow of a Doubt, All Quiet on the Western Front* and *Destry Rides Again* - until the tail end of the decade. But among their B-series, Sherlock Holmes was the studio's tallest tent pole. Other poles - notably, Abbot & Costello and the Maria Montes/ John Hall adventure series - had been taller when they were new, but by the mid-50s they had been banished to theatrical kiddie matinees.

In any event, the test was sufficiently successful [ie, healthy sales; no significant blow back] that a few months later, the company took the next step, selling their Sherlock Holmes films outright. In Summer 1954, James A. Mulvey [he, who with Walter O'Malley, owned the Brooklyn Dodgers, and with Samuel Goldwyn, owned Goldwyn Pictures] bought the series for himself, along with several Universal serials and a few second-tier Walter Wanger productions - and authorized a national release.

With that sale, the Rathbone-Bruce series was now ready for major markets across the country. By fall, the films debuted on the country's most prominent network affiliates - CBS' principal branch in Philadelphia [WCAU], its flagship station in New York [WCBS] and then, in December, over DuMont's Chicago affiliate, WGN-TV. No network would as yet televise a theatrical feature nationally - certainly not a B-picture. But their affiliates, even their flagship stations, were willing to act on their own after seeing the ratings and revenues that independent rivals earned.

In short, within a year, Sherlock Holmes had migrated from independents to three separate network stations in Philadelphia, New York, and Chicago. Within that year, too, Universal had come out of the closet as the ultimate author of the sale, determining that the risk of retaliation from ever-weakening independent theatres and chains, disinclined to fight over B-picture filler, was off-set by the ever-increasing profits from television syndication. Growing TV audiences meant ever-increasing paydays for a studio renting out old films that otherwise had virtually no commercial afterlife.

And yet, it is a sign of the turbulent relations between studios and this new market that Universal still insisted on shielding itself with dummy companies and third parties should they require deniability. Instead of releasing their Holmes films themselves, they - and then Mulvey - outsourced the series to innocuous-sounding companies controlled by an egg-shaped man little known outside the industry.

He is worth our attention. True, Mathew 'Matty' Fox did not keep the Rathbone series alive out of love for Sherlock Holmes. But the series could have found no sharper, better qualified champion. Known for his steel nerves and razor-sharp intelligence, Fox was the consummate Hollywood player - arguably the most important figure in the history of film libraries.

Eventually, Fox would revolutionize the way studios used their vaults, demonstrat-

Figs. 4/5: Reissue Lobby Cards. ©Realart, 1948. Only these two Universal Sherlock Holmes films were ever officially reissued theatrically after the war, usually paired with each other on a double bill.

ing how to use libraries to finance current film production. While a vice president at Universal, he had taken the distribution of old films to a new level, outsourcing the sound library to a company called Realart Pictures in a deal that made millions for Universal. Two Sherlock Holmes films were part of that group, *Sherlock Holmes and the Secret Weapon* and *The Scarlet Claw,* routinely reissued to sub-run theatres and drive-ins at the tail end of the 1940s.

Having masterminded deals that were credited with revitalizing Universal, Fox was now setting up companies of his own, and in 1954 engineered the most spectacular studio sale of the decade. He will show up continually in the Holmes television saga, the hidden hand behind the Rathbone-Bruce broadcasts, as he had been the catalyst for their short-lived theatrical reissue, and the link to the first Holmes series made for TV (in 1954), starring Ronald Howard and H. Marion Crawford.

Had it not been for his elaborate machinations, in fact, it is likely the Universal series would have died in the vaults. The original contracts Universal signed with the Conan Doyle estate stipulated that the company's rights to the stories terminated in 1952 and that "immediately after said date" Universal was to withdraw the film from distribution and destroy all negatives and all exhibition prints. The contracts also contained provisions that specifically forbade TV broadcasts. To quote the agreement for *Terror by Night* (1946), "[Universal] may announce but may not exhibit or dramatize the photoplay by television. [Universal] may announce but not dramatize said photoplay on radio."[4] One function of Matty Fox's web of intermediate companies was to skirt the enforcement of those initial contracts.

Unfortunately, no subsequent literary rights agreement between Universal or Fox's companies and the estate is available, but the few clues that survive indicate that Arthur Conan Doyle's sons simply found themselves lost in the maze that Fox had created. In any case there is no evidence of any litigation directed against Universal-International or Fox's companies; nor is there any evidence that the estate - notorious for its litigious enthusiasms - saw any additional revenues from the television broadcasts.

Regardless, the timing of those broadcasts could not have been better. Matty Fox's Motion Pictures for Television [MPTV] acquired the TV rights from James Mulvey, just as Matty Fox's Western Television Corp [WTC] had bought them from Universal-International, and then sold them to a Matty Fox spin-off, Associated Artists Productions [AAP], run by one of Fox's former business partners. And even as he was selling and bartering

Holmes and the Snake Skin Suits:
Fighting for Survival on '50s Television
Russell Merritt

licenses to stations, the dam was about to break, with top-line Hollywood movies set to flood the airwaves. A few weeks before Holmes' appearance in New York (on 9 September 1954), Fox was engineering his greatest coup, and the most consequential of his many deals: arranging the $25 million sale of Howard Hughes' RKO Radio Pictures to Thomas O'Neil, owner of WOR-TV and two regional networks. With that sale, finally consummated July 1955, O'Neil came into possession of some 760 features that he could then supply to WOR's daily movie program, *Million Dollar Movie*. Treasures included classics like *King Kong, Citizen Kane,* Hitchcock's *Notorious,* John Ford's *The Informer,* films starring Katherine Hepburn and Cary Grant, Fred Astaire musicals, and all the Val Lewton horror films, including *Curse of the Cat People, I Walked with a Zombie,* and *The Body Snatcher.* Fox immediately bought territorial rights for the markets O'Neil didn't control and spun those off to a sub-distributor called C&C Television Corp, which included a window for broadcast over the ABC network. With that, RKO's A-line product became available to every TV station in the country, and other major studios rushed to follow suit. Fearful that if they did not sell off their A-film libraries promptly rivals would beat them to the punch and saturate the market, each studio raced to sell off its top-line "vaulties" at premium rates. Within eighteen months of the RKO sale, every major except Paramount had created prestige packages to be marketed on TV.

This changed the equation for the networks. In the days before the reissue of the Sherlock Holmes series, old movies had been the domain of local stations, whether affiliates or independents. The networks themselves wanted nothing to do with them. As they saw it, it was a battle for control. Network executives like David Sarnoff and William S. Paley feared that film libraries made affiliates less dependent on network feeds, tempting affiliates to bypass expensive network programs to show low-cost movies that the local stations had licensed for themselves and could market to local sponsors [lots of them, as it happened] for greater profits.

But now networks saw the potential for nationwide broadcasts of vintage films that could attract comparable audiences to the ones watching their famous variety shows and live dramas. And at less cost. So, while the Sherlock Holmes series, like other B-film products were permanently banished to late-night shows and matinees, *The Wizard of Oz, King Kong, Top Hat, Gunga Din* and their successors found massive new audiences on network prime-time.

And what became of Holmes in the backwash? In a nutshell, he morphed. From a film personality showcased on TV, he became a TV personality reacting to his Rathbone film prototype. Today, the Sheldon Reynolds TV series starring Ronald Howard and H. Marion Crawford is all but forgotten. But it is of interest both for its remarkable production history and as the first of the post-Rathbone Holmes incarnations. In it, the Universal formula was turned on its head - everything from the portrayals of Holmes and Watson to the Victorian settings and increasingly farcical-macabre stories were meant to stand in contrast to their predecessors.

Fig. 6: "The Case of the Cun-
ningham Heritage," Sherlock
Holmes MPTV, 18 October
1954. An American producer,
a British cast, and a French
crew, at the historic Éclair
studio in Epinay-sur-Seine.

In Howard's Holmes, the high-strung, moody, infallible Rathbone gives way to an absent-minded, impetuous, and non-threatening youngster. Even more remarkable is the new Watson: Bruce's *boobus Britannicus* transformed to Crawford's *astutus Britannicus*. Crawford to this day remains the unsung pioneer of the modern Watson as an intelligent, witty, and bemused companion. In place of Universal's twentieth century London, the TV series returned Holmes to the Victorian era, making a point in the publicity campaign of the care taken in reconstructing Baker Street and its environs. In fact, the wonderfully detailed 221B sitting room was copied from the room Michael Weight created for the celebrated Sherlock Holmes exhibit in the 1951 Festival of Britain.

For Matty Fox, it was a natural progression. MPTV had become the market leader in the distribution of movies on television; now it was time to produce and market actual television programs. Sherlock Holmes followed with him. By the time he underwrote the new Holmes program, Fox already had at least eight new teleplay series in the works, but Holmes proved his most expensive - and most lucrative - property. He contracted with Sheldon Reynolds, a young American producer to provide thirty-nine *Sherlock Holmes* episodes in seven months. The films were to be made at studios in the refurbished Éclair studios at Epinay-sur-Seine, with a French crew and a British cast of unknowns and faded veterans.

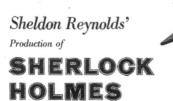

Sheldon Reynolds'

Production of

SHERLOCK
HOLMES

...*Starring Ronald Howard as Sherlock!*

The greatest detective of all time comes to TV ...on film. Here is a series that is backed with one of the most extensive pre-sold audiences in TV history. For almost 70 years the adventures of SHERLOCK HOLMES and his friend Dr. Watson have been thrilling audiences in the great Arthur Conan Doyle books! In the movies...on the stage ...and in daily and Sunday newspapers ...the magic name of SHERLOCK HOLMES always has meant box office! And now — as a TV film show produced by Sheldon Reynolds, creator of "Foreign Intrigue", and starring Ronald Howard, brilliant young English actor— the potential is even greater!

SHERLOCK HOLMES /TV film/ programs, custom filmed for TV) is ready for September airing.

SHERLOCK HOLMES, filmed in Europe, is a natural for local, regional and national spot advertisers!

For A Sure Clue To Increased Business write, wire or phone your nearest MPTV Film Syndication Division:

The series benefited from seasoned American directors and writers and from remarkable behind-the-scene French talent, produced on an historic sound stage. Sacha Kamenka, whose father created the legendary Russian-French Albatros Film Studio, was the stage manager who himself went on to stage manage *Hiroshima Mon Amour* and Jean Anouilh's *Le rideau rouge*. Music was written by Paul Durand, the prolific composer and music arranger for Edith Piaf, among others. And the associate producer was Nicole Milinaire, one of television's first senior female executives, with a reputation for extraordinary efficiency and resourcefulness.[5]

So, Universal B-films gave way to Sheldon Reynolds' B-telefilms. Today we may be struck by the crude look of the Ronald Howard telefilms, especially when compared with the Rathbone productions. The Universals, though cheaply produced, ranked

Fig. 7: Trade ad for Sheldon
Reynolds' Sherlock Holmes
with Matty Fox's MPTV logo.
Broadcasting 12 July 1954

Holmes and the Snake Skin Suits:
Fighting for Survival on '50s Television
Russell Merritt

among the most handsome program pictures ever made. Here, fighting even greater budget restrictions plus the limits of 16mm photography and brutal shooting schedules [one 30-minute episode per every four-day week], the films look quaintly unpolished. Aside from the finely-detailed Baker Street apartment and hallway, the indoor scenery consisted of simple painted flats, indistinct manor rooms that could be reused with minor adjustments, and an all-purpose cobblestone street set up inside the studio to be used with an all-purpose studio hansom cab. Dialogue scenes depended on the bland multiple camera technique that had become standard TV practice by the mid-1950s. Graphically this meant an endless series of choker close-ups, designed for efficiency, but not dramatic nuance.

However, this was not the perception of the series at the time. The first three episodes were particularly well received, even in the pages of *The BSJ,*, and the ratings remained high throughout the first season. The series made headlines for the high prices sponsors were being charged. In New York, the Chase Bank was buying twenty-six weeks for $3,250 per episode; according to *Billboard*, among syndicated series only the Eddie Cantor Show charged more.[6]

Regardless, the series had difficulty finding enough sponsors to sustain a second season. Critics, notably Edgar W. Smith in the pages of the *BSJ*, lost their enthusiasm, and after a season-and-a-half, it ended. By then - Fall, 1955 - Matty Fox was at it again. He mortgaged the Sheldon Reynolds series and sold off syndication rights to a consortium called UM&M, while he unloaded his Universals [along with the rest of his library] to the aforementioned AAP. Like Mr. Toad bouncing in his motor car, he leapt out of film distribution and TV production so he could now focus on his latest pet project: Pay TV. He would prove some thirty years ahead of his time.

With Fox's departure, Holmes' adventures on syndicated television did not exactly come to an end. The Sheldon Reynolds series may have disappeared, but the Universals were endlessly recycled as they were licensed and sub-licensed to one distributor after another. Eventually they even came onto the 16mm educational market, the Universal logos restored. But not until PBS imported the Granada series, thirty years after the Rathbone TV debut, would Jeremy Brett provide Americans a new Holmes created for television.

The escapades that brought about the advent of Holmes' series on television may seem quaint and unnecessarily tortured, but in their day both the Universal reissues and the new Sheldon Reynolds series were shrewd, strategic ways of using the new medium to keep Holmes' memory green. In our own time, media distributors coordinate with services like Amazon, Netflix, and with media conglomerates like Turner Broadcasting and Time-Warner to promote old movies and new TV shows. But the end result is exactly the same: wheeler-dealer antics and quickly-made products co-mingle in a way to bring popular diversion for everyone. What Holmes said of the press in *The Six Napoleons* Matty Fox could say with equal force about television: "a most valuable institution if you only know how to use it." ●

Notes
1. "How to Use TV Films Effectively," Sponsor 19 June 1950, p. 33
2. Pierce (1998), 147-148
3. Broadcasting 19 Apr 1954, p. 34, 36. For the sale of the series to KTTV, Walter Ames, "Sherlock Holmes Films Sold to KTTV," Los Angeles Times, 13 April 1954, p. 26; and Broadcasting, 19 April 1954, pp. 34, 36; for the sale to Cincinnati, Billboard, 8 May 1954, p. 5; for the sale to Tijuana, Billboard 22 May 1954, p. 7.
4. Cited in "Terror By Night," Story File 3709, in summarizing the agreement between Denis P.S. Conan Doyle and Universal Pictures Company, Inc, 24 February 1942.
5. For Milinaire's resourcefulness, Blumberg (2003), 358. For Milinaire's involvement with the Sherlock Holmes series and "Shelly" Reynolds, Milinaire (1974), 145-152, 160-165.
6. For ratings, "The Top Ten Films in Top Ten Markets," Broadcasting 13 June 1955, p. 35 and 9 May 1955, p. 35. For sales, Billboard, 27 Nov 1954; 28 May 1955, p. 10

GO FURTHER

p. 29 **cartoon and newsreel.** Or as filler in a vaudeville show. *Sherlock Holmes Faces Death* opened at the Chicago Oriental opposite a variety show that included Emmy's Madwags and Al Dexter and His Texas Troopers. In Manhattan, the Sherlockian double feature *The Scarlet Claw* and *Sherlock Holmes and the Secret Weapon* backed "9 BIG ACTS!!" at the RKO Jefferson.

As Universal B-pictures, the Holmes series kept colorful on-screen company. Most commonly, the films were paired with Abbott & Costello comedies, exotic adventure pictures starring Maria Montez, or horror films like *Calling Dr. Death* and *The Mad Ghoul*. But not always. In New York *Sherlock Holmes in Washington* opened on the Loews' circuit supporting a Judy Garland musical called *Presenting Lili Mars*. In Chicago, *Sherlock Holmes and the Voice of Terror* ran with a re-run of *Bambi*.

p. 29 **passed into contempt.** John McElwee's blog, Greenbriar Picture Show, provides an excellent, informal overview of the labyrinthine directions both the 20th Century-Fox and Universal Sherlock Holmes films took on television.

Steinbrunner and Michaels (1978) for newspaper reviews of the Rathbone films during their first run.

p. 30... **anywhere in the United States.** Before this, Holmes had appeared only in single episodes of the syndicated series *Your Show Time* and *Suspense*, and in a closed circuit broadcast produced by NBC in November 1937. The BBC series produced in 1951 with

Holmes and the Snake Skin Suits:
Fighting for Survival on '50s Television
Russell Merritt

Alan Wheatley was never shown in the U.S. Haining (1991), 93-97, and Barnes (2008)
McElwee [op. cit.] believes 20th Century Fox's *The Hound of the Baskervilles* (1939)
may have been surreptitiously televised prior to the Universals by Hygo Television Films,
but this has not been confirmed.

p. 30... ***Walter Wanger and Alexander Korda.*** The broadcast of the Wanger and Selznick
films is at the heart of the complaint launched by exhibitors against TV distributor Film
Classics, Inc., cited in Hoyt (2012), p. 213. The titles are named in Davis (2008), p. 226;
but Davis errs in assuming the TV exhibition was directed by Selznick and Wanger. Their
companies had dissolved during the war and had sold off all rights. Cf. Film Classics, Inc.,
Acquires Selznick-Whitney Prints, *New York Times* 19 July 1943, 21.

p. 31... ***for over a year.*** The Chans had been packaged together with a miscellany of
other, unrelated films, the better to disguise their age and their Twentieth Century-Fox
origins. Fox had licensed the Charlie Chan features to a dummy company called Major
Attractions; Major Attractions in turn passed them off to Unity TV Corp., who then
lumped them with sixty British pictures and non-Fox Hollywood films. Cf. Pierce, and
Broadcasting, 15 June 1953, p. 33. Strangely, the names and faces of the actors who
portrayed Chan were omitted from all trade advertizing, most likely in order to blur the
age of the earliest Chans. Most of the licensed Chans were ones that starred Werner
Oland, dating back to the early 1930s; only a few starred the more recent Sidney Toler,
who was still making Chan films after the Second World War. Cf. Unity TV advert,
Billboard, 19 June 1953]

p. 32... ***DuMont's Chicago affiliate, WGN-TV.*** Mulvey's June 11, 1954 agreement with
Universal Pictures is cited in Pierce, fns. 48-49, p. 161. Mulvey, it should be noted, was
not acting on behalf of Goldwyn [who had a strong aversion to television], but was buy-
ing the films for himself, parking them in his holding company, Champion Pictures, Inc.
The broadcasts in Philadelphia, New York, and Chicago were reported, respectively,
in *The Philadelphia Inquirer* television listings, 8 May through 20 Nov 1954; in *The
New York Times* television listings from 9 Sept 1954 through 30 May 1955; and in the
Chicago Tribune television listings from 2 Nov 1954.

p. 33... ***the tail end of the 1940s.*** The best account of Matty Fox's frenetic career is
Hoyt (2012). For Fox's masterminding Universal's deal with Realart, Hoyt, and Pierce
(1998). Pierce speculates that the other ten Rathbone Universals were withheld from
the Realart deal because of story rights complications. Withholding them from Realart
simplified Universal's subsequent selling off the properties outright. [Pierce to author,
6/30/13].

p. 33... **Ronald Howard and H. Marion Crawford.** For Fox's involvement with the Sheldon Reynolds series, Blumberg (2003), though Blumberg's reminiscence should be used with extreme caution.

Nicole Milinaire (1974), the associate producer of the Howard-Crawford Sherlock Holmes series, writes about her encounter with Matty Fox, "[who] did most of his business in bed and hated wearing clothes. "

p. 33... **photoplay on radio."** The story file for "Pursuit to Algiers," signed the same date, with identical provisions, is quoted in Pierce, "'Senile Celluloid,'" fn. 48, p. 161.

Universal was also contractually obligated to destroy its negatives to its serials based on King Features materials, including *Flash Gordon, Buck Rogers,* and *Don Winslow of the Navy.* Happily, it did no such thing and through Matty Fox's machinations made their way safely onto television. Wolper, (2003), 19-20

p. 33... **from the television broadcasts.** Boström (2012), 341-44 includes an intriguing study of the estate's correspondence threatening a lawsuit against Universal for unauthorized screenings of *Woman in Green* in New York in fall 1953. The correspondence is part of Richard Lancelyn Green's Arthur Conan Coyle collection in Portsmouth, England. Although the letters refer to a proposed settlement involving a never-realized Universal television series, there is apparently no mention in the correspondence of the 1954 broadcasts of the Rathbone series.

p. 34... **two regional networks.** The RKO sale to Thomas O'Neil has been widely studied. For recent analysis, Hoyt (2012) and Pierce (1998). For an insider's account, Blumberg (2003)

p. 34... **marketed on TV.** For a succinct account of the snowball effect of the RKO sale, Hilmes (1990), 160-163. The best account of MGM's unique marketing of its old films on television is the Greenbriar Picture Shows blog for *Thirty Seconds Over Tokyo* (2012).

p. 34... **for greater profits.** The fullest account of network battles versus the stations is Hilmes. For deeper economic analysis, Kompare (2005), 48-49

p. 34... **on network prime time.** ABC was the first network to broadcast a series of old films nationwide on prime time, starting with A-list British imports. Cf. *Variety* advert., 7 Sept 1955, p. 41. In spring, 1957 ABC expanded its series to include RKO films culled from the C&C Television package. Cf. advert., *LA Times,* 7 April 1957, p. H7, and *Chicago Tribune,* 7 April 1957, p. N16. For the outcome of the networks' decisions to screen movies nationwide on primetime, Hilmes (1990) 166-167. Also, Edwin Schallert, "TV Poses

Holmes and the Snake Skin Suits:
Fighting for Survival on '50s Television
Russell Merritt

&

Deadly Threat to Movies," *Los Angeles Times.* 2 Feb 1958, p. 20.

p. 35... *1951 **Festival of Britain*** Ruth Voboril's website *Sherlock Howard* contains a wealth of information, including information about Reynolds using Michael Weight's Baker Street set, originally designed for the 1951 Festival of Britain [and now on exhibit at the Sherlock Holmes Pub on Northumberland Street in London].

p. 35 ... ***unknowns and faded veterans.*** Production information on the Sheldon Reynolds series is scanty. Extended international production credits for the crew derive from the internet, including IMDb. Blumberg (2003) and the Ronald Howard article reproduced in *Sherlock Howard* website are almost entirely anecdotal accounts.

p. 56... ***a season-and-a-half, it ended.*** For Edgar W. Smith's gradual disillusion with the series as it became more farcical, compare his lyrical editorial review as the series debuted [*BSJl*, 4/4 (October, 1954) 248-250 and *BSJ*, 5/1 (January 1955), 57-58] with subsequent comments [*BSJ*, 5/4 (October 1955), 244; and 6/3 (July 1956), 184].

p. 36... ***thirty years ahead of his time.*** UM&M, in turn, would sell rights for syndicating re-runs for the Sheldon Reynolds series to MPTV's successor, Guild Films, in 1956. For an astute overview of the obstacles confronting pay TV, Hilmes (1990). For a sympathetic assessment of Matty Fox's pay-TV scheme, Hoyt (2012).
As for the Universals, the labyrinth continued. AAP sold them to United Artists in 1957. For a summary of their post-1950s travels, Greenbriar Picture Show blog.

Books

Sherlock Holmes on Screen
Alan Barnes
(Richmond, VA: Reynolds & Hearn, 2008)

Från Holmes Till Sherlock
Mattias Boström
(Oslo [Norway] Piratförlaget, 2012)

The Television Sherlock Holmes
Peter Haining
(London: W.H. Allen, 1991)

Hollywood and Broadcasting
Michele Hilmes
(Champaign, IL: University of Illinois Press,, 1990)

'Hollywood Vault: The Business of Film Libraries 1915-1960'
Eric Hoyt
(Los Angeles, CA: Doc. Diss., University of Southern California, 2012)

Rerun Nation: How Repeats Invented Television
Derek Kompare
(Routledge, 2005)

Nicole Nobody: the Autobiography of the Duchess of Bedford
Nicole Milinaire
(London: W.H. Allen, 1974)

The Films of Sherlock Holmes
Chris Steinbrunner and Norman Michaels
(Secaucus, NJ: Citadel Press, 1978)

Producer
David Wolper
(NY: Scribner, 2003), 19-20

Extracts/Essays/Articles

Holmes and the Snake Skin Suits:
Fighting for Survival on '50s Television
Russell Merritt

'Total Recall'
Lew Blumberg,
Fridays With Art: Insiders' Accounts of the Early Days of the TV Biz by Some of the Guys who Made it Work
(Burbank, CA: Parrot Communications, 2003), pp. 353-355

'Small Screen, Smaller Pictures: Television Broadcasting and B-Movies in the Early 1950s'
Blair Davis
Historical Journal of Film, Radio, and Television. 28:2 June 2008, pp, 219-38

'"Senile Celluloid." Independent exhibitors, the major studios and the fight over feature films on television, 1939-1956'
David Pierce
Film History. 10/2 (1998) pp. 141-164

Online

Greenbriar Pictures Shows. http://greenbriarpictureshows.blogspot.co.uk/
Sherlock Howard, http://sherlockhoward.homestead.com/

'ELIMINATE ALL OTHER FACTORS, AND THE ONE WHICH REMAINS MUST BE THE TRUTH.'

SHERLOCK HOLMES
'THE SIGN OF FOUR'

Fan Appreciation no.1
Anthony Horowitz, author of *The House of Silk*

Interview by Tom Ue
Photo by Adam Scourfield

Readers should be aware that details of the plot of The House of Silk (2011) *are revealed in the following interview.*

The following interview with Anthony Horowitz looks at the many writing projects for children and adults and across media in which he is actively engaged. It explores his reading, how it informs his creative output and his writing process for *The House of Silk*, the first novel about the mature Sherlock Holmes that is endorsed by the Conan Doyle Estate. This interview gives attention to the novel's double-narrative structure; its questioning of ethics, something that has preoccupied the imaginations of Victorians; and the possibility of a sequel.

Tom Ue: *Congratulations on this thoughtful, informed and ambitious Holmes story! Your credits include the creation of both* Midsomer Murders *(ITV, 1997–) and* Foyle's War *(ITV, 2002–), and you have also worked on* Poirot *(ITV, 1989–),* Collision *(Anthony Horowitz, ITV, 2009) and* Injustice *(Anthony Horowitz, ITV, 2011–). Has working on television affected your thinking about and writing for* The House of Silk?
Anthony Horowitz: Yes – I think it influenced it in many ways. If TV teaches you anything, it's the importance of structure and I couldn't have written *The House of Silk* without very clearly seeing its shape from the start. Also, the pace of the novel is very much directed at a modern, TV-educated audience who generally don't like to wait too long for the next twist or action sequence. Finally, I think *Foyle's War* taught me how to immerse myself in a period – and how to use research to be knowledgeable without being long-winded.

TU: *Do you see a future film in* The House of Silk?
AH: It's possible, I suppose – although it will be difficult with the Robert Downey Jr. franchise still running. To be honest, I'm not very excited about the possibility of a film and I certainly won't write the screenplay!

TU: *Earlier this year, you have ended the immensely successful Alex Rider series. Was it difficult? How do you decide when to end a series?*
AH: I would have been mourning Alex Rider if Sherlock Holmes hadn't come to the rescue! I always knew I'd stop writing Alex after eight or nine books. I was frightened that they'd become formulaic and tired. The Bond novels (which I love) go off quite badly after a bit – and that was the trap I wanted to avoid. It helped that I always said I'd stop when Alex reached 15 years of age. That meant there was a built-in limitation.

Fan Appreciation no.1
Anthony Horowitz, author of The House of Silk

TU: *Tell us about the transition from Alex to Holmes. What is similar and/ or different about the two characters?*
AH: They have no similarities at all that I can think of. Posing this question makes me realize what a huge jump I had to make.

TU: *More generally, what do you see as differences between writing for adults and for children?*
AH: Fewer than you think – and for what it's worth, I hope many teens will enjoy *The House of Silk*. I am interested in pace, in story, in suspense, in surprise ... and this remains the same whoever I'm writing for. When I write, I don't really consider my audience. I'm not writing 'for' anyone exactly. Maybe in the edit, I'll take out complex words if I'm writing for young people. There won't be any sex. And of course, there will usually be a teenaged hero at the centre of the story. But there really aren't so many differences.

TU: *Do you see the Holmes canon as children's literature? What about* The House of Silk?
AH: Holmes appeals to a fantastically wide spectrum of readers – in age, sex, ethnicity, etc. It could be said that with Holmes, as with Professor Challenger, Doyle was appealing to the boy in us all. *The House of Silk* has a dark heart but I hope the story will have an equally wide appeal.

TU: *What made you decide to write a brand new mystery for Holmes?*
AH: I loved the Holmes canon when I was a teenager myself. It was an irresistible commission. Also, I was confident I could do justice to Doyle's creation. This may sound conceited but if I hadn't really believed I could do it, I wouldn't have tried.

TU: *Is your thinking about Holmes affected by recent adaptations? How so?*
AH: I enjoyed the BBC take on Holmes and quite liked the film too. But they had no effect on me at all. Before I began writing, I read all the short stories and the four novels. Everything that I needed to write my book was there.

TU: *Did you feel pressured that* The House of Silk *is endorsed by the Conan Doyle Estate and that this is the first time that the estate gave its seal of approval for a new mature Sherlock Holmes novel?*

AH: Not at all. I insisted that the Conan Doyle Estate should have nothing to do with the writing of the book. I would take no notes from them. I would not show them the finished manuscript. It was really important to me to feel that I was trusted – and to give them credit, they gave me their support but nothing more.

TU: *Your first encounter with the Holmes canon was at the age of 16. Tell us about this experience.*
AH: Well, it was a long time ago. I just loved the mysteries, the world, the friendship. There are some authors – Fleming, Doyle, Dickens, Rowling even – who don't just create stories. They create entire worlds. The pleasure of reading their books is that you get to live in their world. That was what happened when I read Holmes for the first time. It was completely immersive.

TU: *What do you see as being distinctive about Holmes as a detective?*
AH: Forgive me if I don't answer this one. It is both obvious and indefinable.

TU: *You bring in the excellent Victorian writer George Gissing – I say this not just because my Ph.D. is partially about him – in your description of the London poor. To what extent are your novel's setting and subject matter informed by your reading of his realist writing?*
AH: I was delighted to see you had written about Gissing as he is one of my favourite authors. He provided the social conscience of the book – missing, to an extent, from Doyle. If you want to experience the hardship and misery of nineteenth-century life, I can't think of a better source.

TU: *You also present Dickens as a predecessor to Gissing. In his criticism on Dickens, Gissing recognizes that his predecessor offers a softened representation of Victorian Britain. With whom do you identify more closely?*
AH: I also love Dickens. He was the better writer. The humour and optimism of his books has helped him to survive where Gissing – resolutely gloomy – has largely been forgotten. I'm probably closer to Gissing in my own outlook but closer to Dickens in my tastes.

TU: *Why have Watson write* The House of Silk *after 25 years and when both Holmes and Lestrade have died?*
AH: There had to be a reason why we had never heard of *The House of Silk*. It had to contain something dark and scandalous. It therefore fol-

Fan Appreciation no.1
Anthony Horowitz, author of The House of Silk

lowed that Watson probably wouldn't have wanted the book to be published. Also, having an older Watson allowed me to use a more modern idiom (1915 language) and it gave the book a certain poignancy.

TU: *Why have Watson give his account at a time of war?*
AH: It's just the way the dates worked out. I like the idea of this old man in a nursing home, on his own, while the world is in turmoil.

TU: *For one, this double time enables you, I think, to juxtapose and to contrast the views of the older and narrating Watson and his younger self. This is most apparent when the former observes.*
AH: It is curious to reflect now, at the very end of my writing career, that each and every one of my chronicles ended with the unmasking or arrest of a miscreant, and that after that point, almost without exception, I simply assumed that their fate would be of no further interest to my readers and gave up on them, as if it was their wrongdoing alone that justified their existence and that once the crimes had been solved they were no longer human beings with beating hearts and broken spirits. (p. 153)

TU: *Should we be more critical of Holmes? Of Watson? Of Conan Doyle?*
AH: Absolutely not. Watson is not being critical in this passage. It's just that because he's older, he is more prone to analysis … is this not natural? My aim was to write a book that served Doyle and obeyed all his rules. But I didn't want to be slavishly unoriginal. The older voice of Watson allows me to question, very subtly, some things that the books take for granted.

TU: *I wonder, too, if there is a gap between how the older and narrating Watson sees the legal system and how the younger and experiencing Watson sees it. For instance, Watson reflects on Fitzsimmons's death by the end of the novel:*
AH: He was without any doubt a monster but no country can afford to throw aside the rule of law simply for the sake of expediency. This seems even more clear to me now, while we are at war. Perhaps his death was just an accident, though a lucky one for all concerned.

TU: *What do you think?*
AH: You're right. This sort of sentiment seems very much in keeping with an older Watson and allows me to push the envelope a little, so to speak.

TU: *You position this story very precisely in the Holmes timeline. Tell us* *about your decisions here.*

AH: I'm sure Holmes fans will find faults with the timeline although I've done my best to get it right. The important dates are Watson's wedding and Holmes's supposed death, one year after my story ends. But Doyle himself was never that bothered about the fine details. 'Accuracy of detail matters little,' he once wrote. 'What matters if I hold my readers?'

TU: *The novel effectively brings together two seemingly-unrelated mysteries. What made you structure it in this way?*

AH: Thank you for noticing. I had a challenge from the very start. The Holmes novels are about 40,000 words. My publishers wanted 90,000. How could I expand the story and still be true to the sort of structure/framework that Doyle used. The answer was to write two stories but to tie them together in such a way that, hopefully, nobody would see the join.

TU: *The violence behind Ross's murder sets it apart from the stories in the Holmes canon. Tell us about this choice.*

AH: The violence of the murder is necessary for two reasons. It seriously jolts Holmes and makes him question his motives. And it reminds my readers that although I am known for my children's books, this is not one of them.

TU: *Lestrade claims that Ross's death was Holmes's 'fault':*

AH: I warned you about mixing with these children. You employed the boy. You set him on the trail of a known criminal. I grant you, he may have had his own ideas and they may have been the ruin of him. But this is the result.

TU: *To what extent is Holmes guilty in his employment of the Baker Street Irregulars?*

AH: I think that's a question for the reader to answer. And for Holmes.

TU: *Is Holmes, however indirectly, exploiting these children?*

AH: Again, this is not for me to answer.

TU: *Holmes finds an unlikely ally in Moriarty in your novel. What made you bring him in?*

AH: I couldn't have written a Holmes novel without Moriarty. He is just too delicious a character. But having him as the main villain would have been too obvious. I wanted to use him in an unexpected way.

Fan Appreciation no.1
Anthony Horowitz, author of The House of Silk

TU: *Why suggest, perhaps, a more sympathetic aspect to this character?*
AH: See 'The Final Problem'. Holmes had a healthy respect for Moriarty.

TU: *Importantly, Moriarty seems to underestimate Holmes's resourceful-ness when Moriarty gives Watson the key. Is this strategic?*
AH: Does Moriarty really give Watson the key to help Holmes escape or is he perhaps trying to establish a moral position, staking his ground – so to speak? You decide.

TU: *Were you inspired by Edmond Dantès's escape from Alexandre Du-mas's The Count of Monte Cristo (1844) in your thinking about Holmes's? Give us a glimpse of your thought process behind this!*
AH: I have read and enjoyed that book but it didn't influence me. I can't answer this question without giving away how that sequence works. So I won't.

TU: *One of the novel's many red-herrings, for me, is Patrick, the scowling Irish scullery boy. Tell us more about him. How much does he know about the two mysteries?*
AH: Patrick is in his own way a victim. He behaves the way he does be-cause of the way he has been treated by his employer.

TU: *How much does the rest of the household know?*
AH: Everyone knows. Nobody says.

TU: *Although Holmes solves the two mysteries, the novel shows, clearly, that he can neither alleviate the damage done nor bring all the criminals to justice. Tell us more about your decisions behind this resolution.*
AH: I'm not sure Holmes ever sets out exactly to alleviate damage or to seek justice. He solves crimes and that is what he does here.

TU: *What is next for your Holmes?*
AH: I don't intend to write a second Holmes novel. It would end up being compared to the first and might not be as good. I will write a novel set in the same world and it is possible that Holmes might make a fleeting appearance but I worry that a second outing might be little more than cynical.

TU: *What are you working on now?*

AH: I am writing a children's novel, the last volume of my Power of Five series. I am working on a ten-part TV series for ITV. And I am writing a movie of *Tintin*.

TU: *Thank you so much for your time, and for giving us a novel that avoids simple answers! I look forward to reading much more Holmes from you!*
AH: Sorry. But that's it! ●

~~~~~~~~~~

GO FURTHER

Books

The House of Silk
Anthony Horowitz
(London: Orion, 2011)

Chapter
3

Doyle or Death?
An Investigation into
the World of Pastiche

Luke Benjamen Kuhns

→ It was in Beeton's 1887 Christmas Annual where Sir Arthur Conan Doyle published his first story that featured Sherlock Holmes and Doctor John H. Watson. Little did the first consumers know at the time, but they were reading the first story of one of literature's greatest and most recognizable characters. It did not take long for the readers to fall in love with Doyle's characters nor did it take long for other writers to feature Sherlock Holmes in their own stories. Writers had begun to appropriate since at least 1891, three years before Holmes' return from death in 1894. In 1899, Holmes was refashioned for the stage by Doyle and William Gillette in the four-part play titled *Sherlock Holmes*. However, the version written with Doyle was lost in a fire at the Baldwin Hotel along with the original adaptation by Gillette, so he re-wrote most of it himself. Doyle's own son, Adrian, continued this tradition when he contributed his own writings to his father's work and produced *The Exploits of Sherlock Holmes* (1954), where he attempted to tell all of the referenced stories within his father's work, though he never brought this venture to an end.

Sherlock Holmes, and the world Doyle created, has sparked the imagination of many writers who wish to see more of his adventures. From books to film, radio dramas to T.V. series, animated cartoons to comic book adaptations, the continuing adventures of Holmes and Watson's have been ever growing since the late Victorian Era.

In this chapter, we will examine the world of pastiche, while assessing some of the different kinds. From traditional to crossover novels, and finally graphic novelizations, this paper will examine their strengths and weaknesses to determine what works and what, perhaps, does not. In the world's extensive library of pastiche there are, most certainly, gems; but there are also some incredibly outlandish takes written within Doyle's brand. But as Doyle once famously said to William Gillette when he first asked permission to adapt him to theatre, "marry him, murder him, do anything you like."

Pastiche Traditional:

The advent of pastiche and adaptation within different media has brought with it a number of amputations and extensions. Evoking the feel of the original stories by Doyle, the new stories, written under this traditional approach, provide readers with the warm sense of the well known and loved. Some might argue that this can provide new reading material that deepens the world created by Doyle and furthers the Holmes/Watson partnership. However, what it certainly does is perpetuate the brand, widening the opportunity for assiduous readers and fans of Doyle's work to find new material to read within the familiar sitting room.

Often, traditional style stories are written as a homage to Doyle's style, while at times they provide the author with the opportunity to add little bits of their own style into the narrative. This can help keep the stories fresh and exciting.

Take for example Anthony Horowtiz's pastiche *The House of Silk* (2011). This novel kept within the traditional framework of Doyle while at the same time showcasing a darker side of Victorian London than what we saw in Doyle's original stories. It also tweaked with the mythos of Sherlock Holmes as Doctor Watson is blindfolded and taken to a mysterious house where he encounters Professor Moriarty. For Holmes enthusiasts this scene could be a nice nod, while other might view it as tampering with the mystery of Moriarty. However, what works in pastiche writer's favor is simple: Doyle himself con-

Doyle or Death? An Investigation into the World of Pastiche
Luke Benjamen Kuhns

tradicted his own narratives from time to time. We read in *The Valley of Fear* (1915), set before Holmes' Reichenbach Fall, that Watson has some awareness of Moriarty; however, in 'The Final Problem' (1893) Watson has no knowledge of the fiendish Professor. These plot-holes open doors for traditionalists to have a bit of creative fun with their extension stories.

For example, 'The Adventure of the Diamond Jubilee', which featured in my first novella, *The Untold Adventures of Sherlock Holmes* (2012), delves deeper into the criminal empire of Professor Moriarty. However, this story is set after Moriarty's demise and reveals a new threat that has risen from the ashes of late Professor Moriarty, which I further explored in my followup novel *Sherlock Holmes: Studies In Legacy* (2013). In 'The Solved Problem' I take liberties and look into the problem of Watson's 'wives'. Doyle married Watson off in *The Sign of Four* (1890) to Mary Morstan; after 'The Final Problem' Mary seems to disappear as Watson moves back in with Holmes. The plot-holes thicken when Watson seems to be married again in 'The Illustrious Client' (1924) and 'The Blanched Soldier' (1926) to an unnamed woman.

Other traditionalist stories such as the *Seven Percent Solution* (1974) by Nicholas Myers keep canonically in-line but tell a completely different story than that which Doyle did. Myers' focus is set on Holmes' drug addiction and Watson and Mycroft's concern for his health. In this tale it is revealed that Moriarty, Holmes childhood tutor, is not a criminal mastermind, but due to Holmes' drug addiction he turned Moriarty into the fiendish mastermind after traumatic childhood experience. This novel is widely praised by Holmesians despite its altering, entirely, the events in 'The Final Problem' and what would inevitably change the return of Sherlock Holmes in 'The Empty House' (1903).

Though Horowitz, Meyers, and myself keep canonically faithful, we take certain liberties. We also have a certain level of action and suspense that is perhaps more cinematic in its execution than what one would find in Doyle's original tales. Whilst some traditionalist are okay with this tinkering, others view it as problematic. However, there is not a right or wrong way to handle these plot-holes or levels of action and suspense. It is simply for the reader to decide what they like and do not. When writing traditional pastiche it is hugely important that any author understands the context of this era in which Holmes is set. One must understand and know the historical and sociological backgrounds, from the wealthy to the slums, and most importantly one must also know the canon. It it has been taken as an opportunity by the continuing authors of Sherlock Holmes, to work with these inconsistencies. Research, both historically and canonically, is vital and, if not done well, it will damage any traditional pastiche.

Pastiche Crossovers
There are little to no genres that Holmes has not touched. Placing Holmes within a world of magic, science fiction, steampunk, setting him within real historical events, or

even situating him within other pieces of classic literature is not a bad idea. This makes for fun and interesting takes on historical events, twists on classic literature, and opens up a new world for Holmes to explore.

Within some of these genres, it gives the written style a bit more freedom as one need not keep to Doyle's hand - a tone that can be hard to imitate. The narratives do not need to be in Watson's perspective. The effect is that this can widen the universe in which Holmes is in by seeing it through others' eyes.

Not only can these types of books lead new readers back to Doyle, they can lead readers towards other pieces of classic literature or encourage people to explore historical events. As well, having Holmes embrace entirely new genres can pull in a readership that might not ever explore the great detective.

Loren D. Estleman's Dr Jekyll and Mr Holmes (1979) is an example of literary mashups. While Doyle didn't particularly drift into the realm of sci-fi when it came to Sherlock Holmes in 'The Creeping Man' (1923) those elements are there. Estleman is also responsible for Sherlock Holmes Vs Dracula (1978). Both literary mashups feature the detective in a fantastic setting dealing with science and monsters, but what Estleman does is ground the stories in a world that feels very much like the world of Doyle. His understanding of Sherlock Holmes reflects throughout his narratives. While these tales might not be considered 'traditional' in their elements or genre, the tone and pace of these works are. They do bring something unique to the library of pastiche.

There are many books in which Holmes is set within a historical setting, for example Mike Hogan's Sherlock Holmes & Young Winston (2012), Edward Hanna's The Whitechapel Horrors (1992), or Kieran McMullen's Sherlock Holmes & The Irish Rebels (2011). Each of these novels places Holmes in a historical setting, but they do not always follow a traditional approach.

Take Bernard J. Schaffer's Whitechapel: The Final Stand of Sherlock Holmes (2011) for instance. It does not match the writing style of Doyle nor does it flow canonically or keep inline with the characteristics of Sherlock Holmes, Doctor Watson, Irene Adler, Mary Morstan, or Inspector Lestrade. In Schaffer's take on the Whitechapel murder and the mystery of Jack the Ripper, he offers an unsettling tale of mental instability, drug addiction, homosexuality, vulgarness, and infidelity. From a traditionalist point of view, this book does everything 'wrong'. This might be a Sherlock Holmes story set in Victorian London, but the approach is in no way an extension of Doyle's work. As is always the case it is up to the reader to decide what they like and do not like. Traditionalists may have trouble with this particular novel, but it is it has a lot to offer, not as an extension but in the ideas that he plays with throughout the narrative.

Then there are some novels that break away from the traditional setting. P.C. Martin's Steampunk Holmes (2012) situates Sherlock Holmes, Doctor Watson, and Sherlock's sister Mycroft into a steampunk universe. The most unique thing about this narrative is that not only does it places Holmes into an entirely different genre, but it also mash-

Doyle or Death? An Investigation into the World of Pastiche
Luke Benjamen Kuhns

es Holmes with yet another literary classic as the plans for Captain Nemo's ship, the Nautilus, has been stolen and Holmes must find them. Elements from Verne and Doyle are what Martin uses to crafts this unique narrative where Doctor Watson possesses a mechanical arm and Sherlock Holmes rides a souped up motorcycle called The Widow.

The prevalent worry is that some stories may be redundant, and that too many authors are doing the same story. Sherlock Holmes can only battle Jack the Ripper or Count Dracula so many times. And when trying to place Holmes within a 'new' genre or setting, there is the problem that the story could be too outlandish.

The other concern is that some crossovers lack originality as some are simply retelling other pieces of classic literature or historical events. This means you will learn nothing new by the end. It is also a problem in that some might see that there is too much uprooting and Holmes and Watson are at their best in their own element.

Pastiche Graphic Novels
Graphic novels or 'comic books' have a bad-rap. There is the misconception that the stories within these illustrated pages are simply juvenile and made for the illiterate. However, when some of the top grossing films in history are based of graphic novels one has to step back and ponder, 'hold on, maybe there is something there!"

Like any piece of literature, graphic novels tell stories of growth, pain, love, loss, and anything else that a writer wishes to write about. The idea that because it is a story with pictures means that it is 'dumbed down' is false. The combination of written word and visuals, such as what can be seen in the steampunk graphic novel 'Moriarty', opens up the readers mind and lets them enter a story in a new and different way. Both written and visual elements compliment each other. Like any painting - they set the tone differently from a written story.

Sherlock Holmes graphic novels fall into the same genres. Both formats do not shy away from a certain genre. For example in Marcie Klinger's and my *Sherlock Holmes and the Horror of Frankenstein* (2013) we combine Doyle with Mary Shelley's gothic horror in a Hammer horror-like story. Much like Estleman's novel *Dr Jekyll and Mr Holmes*, *The Horror of Frankenstein* grounds the story in a realistic world whilst giving Holmes and Watson a truly monstrous foe. While the story is not meant to be taken as an extension, it is a tribute to both crime fiction and classic horror.

What makes graphic novels unique is the visual medium. It is a brand new way of understanding a story and it gives writers and illustrators a chance to bring Holmes to life in a way we may not have seen before. To be able to see Holmes' expression and body language while he investigates, to see the urgency as he and Watson race to stop a villain, to see the surprise and excitement live is magical. Much like film, graphic novels are an artistic media that allows you to enter into a story in a fresh way. Take Edginton and Culbard's graphic novel series for example. Their take on *A Study in Scarlet (2010)* is beautifully illustrated and true to Doyle's novel. The tone in each panel is drenched in mystery as the adventure presses on. The story pops in a bold way. Martin Powell's *Hound of the Baskerville (2013)* is another graphic novel that purveys a grim and gothic atmosphere that is most suitable for this original tale.

To non-graphic novel readers, the style could appear confusing if one does not know how to follow the speech bubbles. Moreover, graphic novels, in general, already have a limited audience, and the Holmes brand contributions become a niche within a niche. Also some of the mystique of the written world is arguably lost as it is drawn. And of course, if the illustrations are not of good quality it can be very distracting and take away from the narrative.

Conclusion

The doors are wide open for authors to continue to explore the world Doyle created in Holmes/Watson. No specific style of pastiche is meant to replace what Doyle has done. Often even the worst pastiche was written purely out of one's love for the characters. There is a rich heritage and wealth of material for fans and enthusiasts to read and enjoy. From traditional novels to crossovers and graphic novels, all of these media are great ways of diving deeper into the world of Holmes. It is important to note that Doyle himself cared little for Holmes - this makes some of the most outlandish types of pastiche non-offensive. Doyle had such a cavalier attitude towards his first literary success. To a degree, readers and writers should be open to the spectrum. Pastiche, in general, is simply a writer's way to pay homage to something they love and admire. No matter what style of pastiche one is approaching with Holmes/Watson the importance of canonical/historical/sociological/genre knowledge is vital to crafting an engaging and well-told story. ●

Acknowledgements

Sherlock Holmes has become a very big part of my life and there are many people who deserve thanks. So, a big thank you to Claire Ellul, whose valuable input was instrumental to the birth of this article, and to Tom Ue for putting this book together. The game is on!

Doyle or Death? An Investigation into the World of Pastiche
Luke Benjamen Kuhns

~~~~~~~~~~~~

GO FURTHER

Books

The Exploits of Sherlock Holmes
Adrian Conan Doyle & John Dickson Car
(London: J. Murray, 1954)

The House of Silk
Anthony Horowtiz
(New York: Little, Brown & Company, 2011)

The Untold Adventures of Sherlock Holmes Holmes
Luke Benjame Kuhns
(London: MX Publishing, 2012)

Sherlock Holmes: Studies In Legacy
Luke Benjamen Kuhns
(London: MX Publishing, 2013)

Sherlock Holmes and the Horror of Frankenstein
Luke Benjamen Kuhns & Marcie Klinger
(London: MX Publishing, 2013)

The Seven Percent Solution
Nicholas Meyers
(Boston: E.P. Dutton & Co., 1974

Dr Jekyll and Mr Holmes
Loren D. Estleman
(New York: Doubleday, 1979

Sherlock Holmes Vs Dracula
Loren D. Estleman
(New York: Doubleday, 1978)

My Evening With Sherlock Holmes
Gibson & Green
(London: Ferret Fantasy, 1981)

Steampunk Holmes
P.C. Martin
(London: MX Publishing, 2012)

Sherlock Holmes & Young Winston
Mike Hogan
(London: MX Publishing, 2012)

The Whitechapel Horrors
Edward Hanna - 1992 - Carroll & Graf Pub

Sherlock Holmes & The Irish Rebel
Kieran McMullen
(London: MX Publishing, 2011)

Whitechapel: The Final Stand of Sherlock Holmes
Bernard J. Schaffer
(https://www.createspace.com: CreateSpace Independent Publishing Platform, 2011)

A Study in Scarlet
Doyle, Edginton, and Culbard
(London: SelfMadeHero, 2010)

Hound of the Baskerville
Doyle & Martin Powell
(Milwaukie: Dark Horse, 2013)

The Sherlock Holmes Micellany
Roger Johnson & Jean Upton
(Gloucester: History Press, 2012)

Fan Appreciation no.2
Ellie Ann Soderstrom, author of
Steampunk Holmes: Legacy of the Nautilus

Interview by Tom Ue
Photo by Ellie Ann Soderstrom

Tom Ue: *Congratulations on the publication of* Steampunk Holmes: Legacy of the Nautilus (2013) *interactive book, and thanks for hours of iPad enjoyment! Tell us about your work with Noble Beast.*

Ellie Ann Soderstrom: I spend most of my time answering questions. 'What are interactive books?' 'Will it work on my PC?' 'Are you coming out with more books?' 'When are you coming out with *real* books?' 'Have you seen my sippy cup?' Wait … that last question usually comes from my toddler. But this is such a new genre that most people don't know what the heck I'm talking about when I refer to enhanced digital books (EDBs), which is part of the challenge of pioneering a new genre. It's hard work to break the dirt and plant the seeds – but we've already seen great success with *Steampunk Holmes*, a great 'harvest', and we plan on continuing this journey.

I'm currently working on acquiring contracts with authors to turn their works into EDBs. It's been so fun working with authors, they're a creative, weird (I like weird), and really hardworking bunch. Publishing companies, on the other hand … *strangles pillow*

TU: *How did the idea of a book on app come about?*
EAS: Have you ever been reading a book, read about a device or character, and really wished you could see it? Or when the story is talking about Mr So-and-So taking the Ashenghost Road to Smothsonian Monastery but he stops at the Underhill Winery first, and you wish you could see where he is on a map? Or, have you ever wished for a corresponding soundtrack or sound effects for the story? We simply wished for these things as we were reading – so then we created it. Ten years ago if we wished for it we wouldn't have had the hardware to create it (on one device) but now, *holla!* The iPad and other hardware are here!

TU: *This project was in development for two years. What are some of the challenges that it faced?*
EAS: This project has faced more challenges than climbing up the Cliffs of Insanity without Fezzik the Giant.

Mostly, the challenge was in development. It took the developers a long time to get the software right, because they all had day jobs and couldn't devote eight hours every day to making it become a reality.

TU: *The project was successfully funded by Kickstarter. Tell us about the response to this project.*

Fan Appreciation no.2
Ellie Ann Soderstrom, author of *Steampunk Holmes: Legacy of the Nautilus*

EAS: We had an overwhelming positive response. Support came from everywhere – Baker Street Babes, Arthur Conan Doyle Foundation and even Neil Gaiman gave us a retweet! We earned far more than our projected amount, which was thrilling.

Based on its success, we want to fund the artwork for all our projects this way. It not only lets us pay fantastic artists what they deserve, but it also gives us an instant fan base, which is greatly appreciated.

TU: *An app involves readerly engagement on so many levels. How did you balance between the music, the text, the visuals and the hypermedia elements in* Steampunk Holmes?
EAS: We do it by centring everything around the text. All the enhancements are optional. You don't have to press each hyperlink, you don't have to interact with the map, you don't have to play the music – but they're all there if you prefer them. Some people are more visual than others. Me, I love the audio portions, music and sound effects (the interactive graphic book app, *Anomaly* (Anomaly Productions, 2012) is a good example of great audio portions).

TU: *Is there anything about an app book that you wish that you could implement but that isn't realistic?*
EAS: Smell-O-Vision, of course! It'd be amazing to have the scent of a fire, the fragrance of a rose, or warm baked cookies coming out of the oven as it was happening in the book. We're so connected to our sense of smell – it'd be fun to connect with it in a book.

TU: *In addition to working for Noble Beast, you are also a prolific writer.*

How do you balance the roles?
EAS: By following Sherlock Holmes's example: I focus on one thing wholeheartedly, finish it, and then move on to the next. I rarely multitask. It's amazing how much you can get done in two hours, when you're focused. I have to stay pretty organized, so I can just jump into a project when I need to and know where I'm at. But I like to keep my writing time regular – to write or edit at least 1,200 words per day so that I can stay in that 'storyworld'.

TU: *Do you identify with your creative writing or your work for Noble Beast more closely?*
EAS: I identify with my writing more closely. It's part of who I am, and I couldn't leave it behind.

TU: *In what ways have these different roles informed each other?*
EAS: Being on the publishing side of things has taught me so much about how to write books that sell. It's taught me a lot about finding your audience and focusing on them. My work is so much stronger now that I've zeroed in on my audience.

TU: *Let's talk more about Holmes. What do you see as some of the factors behind this surge of creative projects on Holmes in recent years?*
EAS: It hasn't been in the public domain that long, so we're just starting to see the surge of creations inspired by his character.
There's something very timeless about Sherlock Holmes and Watson. It appeals to any age. I remember reading my first Sherlock Holmes book at 12 years old, and being so engrossed in the story that I took the book with me everywhere. Last year I reread the canon, and was just as engrossed as ever. It's just plain good writing, characters, and you *need* to keep turning pages to find out whodunit. People in the entertainment business recognize that, and have put their money behind making his stories.

TU: *Having worked on a Steampunk version of Holmes, and written some fiction yourself, what do you see as the appeal of this genre?*
EAS: First of all, the characters. The utterly amiable and empathetic Watson, and the spectacular and exotic Holmes. Their camaraderie and dependence on each other keeps a constant state of micro-tension.
Then, there are the mysteries. In 'The Speckled Band' (2003; Vol. 1), it says, 'He refused to associate himself with any investigation that did not tend towards the unusual, and even the fantastic.' There's great appeal to

Fan Appreciation no.2
Ellie Ann Soderstrom, author of *Steampunk Holmes: Legacy of*

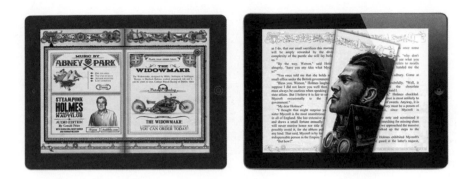

reading about something extraordinary.

Lastly, I'd say that the humour and wit break the ice on the grim and sometimes grotesque cases. If something makes you laugh, it covers a multitude of errors or mistakes in the text.

TU: *What are your major influences?*
EAS: C. S. Lewis, Neil Gaiman and George Washington Carver.

TU: *It's so great to see a writer who maintains such a lively presence on and who productively engages with social media. How important do you see this to being a writer?*
EAS: I don't think it is essential for writers to have a strong social media presence – it's only important for them to write good books. However, I know that I've sold more books through Facebook than any distribution or ad campaign.

I just love interacting with people and getting to know my readers. I like hearing feedback. I like learning things from other writers online. I like meeting new people. Social media is important to me as a writer, it's like a big eternal cocktail party. And I love cocktail parties.

TU: *In what ways do you think that this has changed authorship and the circulation of ideas?*
EAS: It gets you access to more information. As an example, I was about to write a scene that takes place in a coal mine, so I posted on Facebook that I would like to talk to someone who has worked as a coal miner, and I instantly got two responses, and was able to hear first-hand accounts of what it is like in the mines. This improved my writing.

It's phenomenal to be able to access that kind of information.
Another way I think this has improved the circulation of ideas is collaboration. When you need a partner or artist or animator for your work, it's so much easier to get access to them, and instantly see their work. This

keeps you safer from fraud and gives you the ability to pick the right artist for the job.

TU: *What are you working on now?*
EAS: I'm producing a fantasy series for Noble Beast called *Shotguns and Sorcery,* by Matt Forbeck. I love the team we've collected and am really excited to see the excellent enhanced book that it becomes.

I've also finished the first draft to my next novel, *Girls and Boys: A Post Apocalyptic Fairy Tale.* I'm editing it, then I'll send it to editors and beta readers, and hope to publish it in 2014. It's about a backwoods village where the gender roles are reversed, and a girl must journey to the next mountain to kidnap a writer, in order to save her village. It's a comedy, and has been so much fun to write!

TU: *What is next for* Steampunk Holmes?
EAS: We're coming out with *Steampunk Holmes: Frankenstein* next! Our author and artist are hard at work creating it. It's going to be an exciting interactive book.

TU: *Thanks so much for your time, and we look forward to much more Holmes!*

EAS: Thanks so much for having me and asking such astute questions. ●

GO FURTHER

Books

Steampunk Holmes: Legacy of the Nautilus
Noble Beast
(Minneapolis: Noble Beast, 2013)

The Complete Sherlock Holmes, Volumes I and II
Arthur Conan Doyle
Kyle Freeman (ed.) (New York: Barnes and Noble Classics, 2003)

Chapter
4

Sherlock Holmes, Fan Culture and Fan Letters

Jonathan Cranfield

→ **What would lead an individual to compose a letter for the attention of a fictional character? This chapter will argue that the answer can be found within a paradigm shift in the perception of popular culture that has occurred slowly over the last two hundred years and which is in the process of being mapped by the emerging discipline of fan studies.**

Ghislaine McDayter has argued in her monograph *Byromania and the Birth of Celebrity Culture* (2009) that fan behaviour in the eighteenth and nineteenth century was habitually depicted as occurring around the fringes of mainstream consumption and was tainted by intermingled notions of madness, effeminacy and dangerous, radical energy. As such, it fell within the purview of the psychiatrist and the policeman rather than the cultural critic. Yet, readers of this volume (and the series to which it belongs) will have encountered sufficient evidence that modern variants of this behaviour have made the significant transition from margin to mainstream. The multimedia persistence of contemporary pop-culture phenomena demonstrates that, in one sense, the lunatics have taken over the asylum. Fan behaviour that attempts (more or less seriously) to take an active part in shared, imaginary worlds is no longer an epiphenomenal embarrassment to the cultural products that inspired them. Instead, fan participation is encouraged and often written-through the products themselves. These developments have by no means produced uniform results and fan culture is itself riven with hierarchical distinctions between what Matt Hills calls 'resistant' or 'complicit' species of fan activities. 'Resistant' fan culture objects to its own marketization or commodification by the culture industry whereas 'complicit' fan culture makes no such distinctions. To illustrate this distinction in rather crude terms, the 'resistant' fan would risk copyright infringements by actively cutting and collaging the constituent parts of a television show or film whilst the 'complicit' fan would consume officially licensed memorabilia and communicate through designated online discussion boards. Nevertheless, the fundamental problem facing fan studies lies in how to understand the long transitional stages between, say, the treatment of 'Byromania' in the early 1800s and contemporary manifestations of Sherlockiana. By focusing on one particular activity – the writing of fan letters to Sherlock Holmes – which has occurred continuously from the 1890s until the present day, it is possible to observe how particular characteristics of early letter writers presaged and shaped the inchoate language of fan participation and interaction. This is not to say that all letters beginning 'Dear Sherlock Holmes ...' accord to precisely the same psychological and cultural specifications but, in their very variety, they herald the coming multiverse of Sherlockian fan phenomena.

No seminar on the Sherlock Holmes stories is complete without one ill-prepared student asking, in halting terms, 'so, was he *real*, then?' At first glance, the distinction between 'fiction' and 'reality' seems insultingly simple; yet, any readers' consumption of literature has always entailed a creative and subjective treatment of that distinction. The unfeigned confusion of the unfortunate student finds its counterpoint in the ironically-charged 'game playing' of many Sherlockians who speak and write about Sherlock Holmes as if he really existed. As recorded by Andrew Lycett's chapter 'The Strange Case of the Scientist who Believed in Fairies', the inability to critically distinguish fact from fiction was also one of the many accusations (ranging from basic gullibility to full-blown insanity) faced by Arthur Conan Doyle when he publically unveiled his long-held

Sherlock Holmes, Fan Culture and Fan Letters
Jonathan Cranfield

psychical and folkloric beliefs in the wake of World War I. From this perspective, the Sherlock Holmes phenomenon suffered from the unusual fate of being tainted by fanatical lunacy at *both* ends when usually only the fans themselves had found their sanity and discriminatory skills questioned. In this way, unusually porous divisions between fact and fiction became a defining quality of Conan Doyle's legacy into the twentieth and twenty-first centuries.

In the most compelling recent piece of Sherlockian criticism, Michael Saler has eloquently argued against the prevalent idea that, in the early twentieth century, there was a fundamental opposition between modernity and 'enchantment'. The common critical-historical narrative of this period (as adumbrated by Saler) is that the 'pessimistic' view of many late-nineteenth and early-twentieth-century intellectuals (exemplified by Max Weber's discussion of the 'disenchantment of the world') 'was the consequence of capitalist, instrumental rationality and the growth of the bureaucratic state'. According to this narrative, the decay of older, magical or animistic ways of viewing the world were eroded both by the darkening tenor of the historical moment and by the advent of technocratic modes of state and globalized corporate power. However, in response to this age of 'positivism and materialism', argues Saler, many people found new solace in rearticulating the magical and fantastic traditions of western culture. It is simply that their experiences were not reflected by the dominant intellectual tone of the period or by 'official' cultural narratives about artistic modernism. As a consequence, they were left out of the historical record. The business of cultural consumption (whether reading, watching or listening) was, for many people, a far from serious occupation. Rather than being indicative of higher or intellectual thought, culture instead represented a kind of 'play'. Early Sherlockian fan culture belonged to precisely this tradition, a tradition that derived pleasure from treating the ephemeral with utmost seriousness and serious subject matter with discordant levity. As Ronald A. Knox famously wrote in his 'Studies in the Literature of Sherlock Holmes': 'If anyone objects that the study of Holmes literature is unworthy of scholarly attention, I might content myself with replying that to the scholarly mind anything is worthy of study, if that study is through and systematic.' In an age of rationality, playfulness could best be preserved beneath the protective veneer of seriousness. In this way, early-twentieth century consumers became increasingly familiar with creative and progenitive forms of engagement with popular culture. Set against these historical trends on the one hand and the Herculean labours of Knox on the other, the writing of fan letters can be seen less as expressions of individual insanity or 'hysteria' than a way to playfully explore protean notions of interactivity and role-playing.

The assumption that 'fans' could be directly equated with 'fanatics' lead to their marginalization but also their infantilization. Their apparent enthusiasm, solipsism and emotional fragility was enough evidence for Theodor Adorno to condemn jazz fans of the 1930s as 'forcibly retarded' practitioners of 'childish [...] primitivism'. These views accord with those of Sigmund Freud who, in 'Creative Writers and Daydreaming', described creative writers as under-developed specimens whose imaginations had not fully matured beyond the playroom: 'The creative writer does the same as a child at play. He creates a world of phantasy which he takes very seriously.' The desire to inhabit imagined or fantastical worlds is, in this way, rooted in the satisfaction of infantile fantasy as much as it is in the shared infancy of our pre-modern past. However, despite the ceaseless march of the same mordant cultural trends described by Weber, the chapters in this volume demonstrate that contemporary culture provides an ever-increasing abundance of opportunities for fans to achieve precisely this kind of transcendence. Online communities, wiki encyclopaedias, board games, video games, live-action role play and cosplay, have all augmented the more traditional multimedia platforms through which fandom can be expressed. Perversely, just as the utilitarianism of late-modernity planed away older notions of enchantment, so the culture industry became increasingly innovative at providing escape hatches through which weary subjects could escape into imagined worlds. The cultural landscape of Conan Doyle's 1890s was well-equipped to commodify literary works and to enable fans to effectively immerse themselves into their world through stage adaptations, posters, postcards, games, costumes, advertisements, figurines and costumes. Trawling further back through the annals of literary commodification and marketization, we find similar profusions accompanying Samuel Richardson's *Pamela* (1740) and J. W. von Goethe's *The Sorrows of Young Werther* (1774). Those wishing to associate themselves with either of these totemic fictional figures were spoilt for choice amongst bootlegged merchandise such as playing cards, replica Werther pistols, and bespoke outfits which allowed individuals to style themselves as their preferred fictional protagonist. The obsession that attends the minutiae of Benedict Cumberbatch's outfits in the BBC's recent *Sherlock* series (Mark Gatiss and Steven Moffat, 2010–) and the rise of 'Sherlock chic' is thus historically rooted in the perpetual belief that reading the text alone will not satisfy a voracious and obsessive readership. The task of producing memorabilia and merchandise has been rendered legitimate by its incorporation into the business of corporatized culture production. The copyright legislature that protects the intellectual property of authors has become dwarfed by the system of 'trademarking' which perpetually guards ownership of the mass-production of their most famous images, tropes and phrases.

Participation in any of these activities requires fans to make some kind of compromise with hard-line distinctions between fact and fiction, between reality and Freudian 'phantasy'. This does not mean, of course, that fans all *believe* (in the straightforward sense of the word) that Sherlock Holmes was real; rather, in most cases, any 'belief' results from a wager where they are prepared to risk being made to look and feel ridiculous in return for a yield of the infantile pleasure described by Freud. We are all governed by a fear of seeming foolish in the eyes of others and few actions stimulate this particular anxiety like being caught out in a moment of childish play. A child has no reason to hide his phantasies but grown-ups, aware of the burdens of adulthood, are conscious

Sherlock Holmes, Fan Culture and Fan Letters
Jonathan Cranfield

Fig. 1: The 'unofficial' Sherlock Holmes board game
221B Baker Street, originally
released in 1975 by Gibsons
Games (Courtesy of Jona-
than Cranfield).

of the compulsion 'not to go on phantasying any longer' on the grounds that such day-dreams are 'childish' and 'unpermissable'. The risk is the same now for a teenager playing air guitar in their bedroom as it was for middle-aged men donning deerstalkers in the 1960s or those taking on the mantle of Sherlock Holmes through other media such as board games or video games.

With all of this in mind, there remains the question of where the early-twentieth-century writer of fan letters found themselves within these shifting cultural tides. What was at stake in their production, delivery and reception? The evolution of the Sherlockian fan letter can provide a microcosmic study in the slow legitimization and eventual commodification of fan phenomena. From their early stages where they were seen as psychological curiosities that largely conformed to the Freudian theory of underdevelopment or, worse, plain imbecility, they increasingly found willing recipients in the shape of both individuals and institutions who were ready to 'play' along and reinforce the security of the fantasy.

The first practical question facing these correspondents was where to send their compositions; into whose in-tray did they arrive? In the introduction to his edited collection *Letters to Sherlock Holmes* (1985) Richard Lancelyn Green explained that

> Sir Arthur Conan Doyle was the chief recipient, but letters also found their way to various addresses in Baker Street, to Scotland Yard, and to people such as Dr Joseph Bell and William Gillette who shared certain attributes of the great detective.

Conan Doyle's death in 1930 simplified matters and meant that the greater proportion of fan letters were now sent directly to the address '221B Baker Street' which Doyle had innocently invented in 1887's *A Study in Scarlet*. With no 'real' address to receive the letters, there began a scramble from several parties to bring it into being. In a pleasing statement of Holmes's abilities to transcend his imaginative origins, '221B Baker Street' was a fiction that gave birth to a reality, albeit one attended by considerable confusion and argument. From 1933, the Abbey Road Building Society (later, the Abbey National) assumed ownership over the newly-designated 221 Baker Street (a property which had formerly belonged to York Place) and began to receive most of the letters. In subsequent decades, writes Thomas Bruce Wheeler in *Finding Sherlock's London*, the Sherlock Holmes Museum, Abbey National and Westminster Council have all contested their claim to the address and thus for the right to respond to the correspondence as they saw fit. The fact that Westminster Council eventually permitted the Sherlock Holmes Museum to assume ownership of the '221B' address, despite residing elsewhere in the normal numerical sequence of properties, is an example of how the real world began to shape itself to the demands of obsessive fandom and its consequent financial benefits.

Most of the letters sent to 221B Baker Street after 1933 were done so in the 'certain knowledge that a reply [would] be sent' due to the administrative efforts of the Abbey

National which famously maintained a part-time secretarial post solely for processing these letters, responding to them and maintaining the archive from which Green would later draw his material. The vast majority of these letters appear to take pleasure from assuming the well-established role of the wronged client so familiar from the stories. We find, for example, requests for assistance in the famous disappearance of 'frogman Crabb' in 1956, reports of Moriarty's continued existence in a Damascus pub, and several enquiries into Holmes's tastes in tobacco, music, lovers, literature and travel destinations. One question, though, is returned to multiple times in different ways: 'Are you real?'; 'How do you live?'; 'Are you dead?'; 'Are you a fake?' These letters represented tentative calls into the unknown, a loose network of fans broadcasting signals on a test frequency that would become increasingly populous and congested in the years to come. They were often querulous, self-doubting and sometimes betrayed an explicit sense of their own potential ridiculousness. Wayne Preston from Winnipeg began his question by wondering '[w]hy would a logical and reasonable teenager write to an obviously long-dead person such as you?' The responses produced by the Abbey National secretaries were similarly playful and carefully kept up the pretence that Holmes was real but had retired to the Sussex Downs and was thus unreachable. Green notes that the post was filled by individuals who nurtured a passion for the stories and who could 'sustain the correspondence' with 'good humour'. Such letters correspond with Saler's description of 'ironic' enchantment but what about letters that were addressed to 'Scotland Yard' or 'The Metropolitan Police'? These suggest a somewhat different form of fan activity, further removed from the dialogic, collaborative medium of those collected by Green.

A collection of letters addressed in this way forms part of the Metropolitan Police records at Kew's National Archive. As one might expect, their responses were rather less playful than those provided by the game-players of Baker Street:

The Chief Clerk's standardized, type-written response with its invocation of higher authority ('I am directed ...') and its brisk refusal to take any part in any whimsy, is evidence of Saler's views on the disenchanting effect of bureaucratic power. In these cases, where the 'belief' was generated entirely from a single participant in the dialogue, it is tempting to impute even less clear distinctions between fact and fiction on the part of the authors and to look more closely into the underlying psychology of their appeals to Holmes. These letters clearly betray less overt irony and self-questioning; moreover, the problems presented for Holmes's solution are more clearly rooted in the writer's own psychological need. One such letter was sent in 1917 from Timothy Kozynitch Bogdarenko, a disenfranchised Russian revolutionary mystic who believed that Sherlock Holmes 'alone [...] [was] able to reveal and elucidate my prophetic philosophy'. The letter was written in borderline-illegible, handwritten Russian and had to be painstakingly transcribed by a police translator before

Sherlock Holmes, Fan Culture and Fan Letters
Jonathan Cranfield

it could be responded to. Bogdarenko asserted that when he first 'encountered' the Sherlock Holmes stories, he 'accounted it a mythological chronicle' but that he had then 'conclusively established that this personage in fact exists at the present time'. His prophetic philosophy, which was apparently sufficiently bizarre or heretical to have its author banished to the remote town of Kursk, forecast the 'downfall of imperialism and capitalism in general on the earth' and had apparently already been sent to the 'Chief of Police in Stockholm', 'Emperor Wilhelm', 'the State Congress at Washington' and the 'Chief of New York Police'. Amongst all these state and judicial powers, though, Sherlock Holmes was the totemic figure capable of legitimizing and propounding the author's ideas. He provided balm for the wounded narcissism of the fantasist who believed himself to be in possession of the key to all mythologies and on the brink of achieving world power.

The second letter bears out Freud's assertion that, whilst adult fandom entails a regression or retreat from the responsibilities of adulthood, so a child's is determined by 'a single wish – one that helps in his upbringing – the wish to be big and grown up [...] in his games he imitates what he knows about the lives of his elders'. Bearing this in mind, 14-year-old Leslie Wood wrote to Sherlock Holmes in 1931 *via* the Metropolitan Police to ask politely 'Whether Sherlock Holmes [...] is still alive and what is his address?' Despite 'only being 14', the boy 'ha[d] always taken an interest in crime and criminals', had formed 'a detective agency' with his 'chum' and wondered 'whether you have to pass examinations or have a license to be private detective?' Here, Holmes's blessing would confer proper authority upon the acting-out of grown-up fantasies. The myriad personal dilemmas, manias and dissatisfactions that lead adults to compose this kind of 'naive' letter (as opposed to the 'ironic' variety on display in Green's collection) were here condensed into this single wish. Suspension of disbelief, then, could simultaneously serve to facilitate both the childhood *push* for responsibility and the adult *flight* from it. Even from these brief examples, we can see that fan letters offer a succinct summation of the psychological and cultural forces that determined the broader coordinates of nascent fan culture. In the letters addressed to Baker Street we find the desire for a playful, inter-subjective and immersive experience that would come to characterize the current modes of fan consumption and which found willing respondents. Whilst it would be easy to push this notional distinction between 'naive' and 'ironic' believers towards the status of a hard-line opposition, this is far from easily performed. While noting their different characteristics, it is impossible to ever fully separate them. According to Saler, 'irony provides a ludic space in which reason and imagination cavort' and this shield proved sufficiently effective to create the whole contemporary edifice of Sherlockiana. Yet, Edgar W. Smith's 'Introduction' to the first issue of the *Baker Street Journal* (the key organ of Sherlockian scholarship) from 1946 asserted that '[n]o other man has ever been so honoured before [...]; no other times have offered quite so full a flavour of the stuff of which our dreams are made'. From this quote we may determine that, even within the highly sophisticated language game of Sherlockian scholarship, the intimate phantasies, dreams and fears of the players are still at stake. It is only their ability to obscure this fact more successfully that distinguishes them from the likes of Bogdarenko or Wood, who found their appeals mercilessly shut down by the Police's Chief Clerk.

The appeal of a perpetual 1895 for generations of twentieth-century readers described by *The Strand Magazine*'s literary editor H. Greenhough Smith as 'war-tried' is not difficult to fathom. However, it is interesting to consider the stories a little more ahistorically and to examine their intrinsic qualities which may have encouraged these attempts at fan participation. Some explanation may be found in the narrative structure of the stories themselves. Upon examination, many stories repeat a particular early scene that can be made to resemble and reinforce the dynamic of fan letters' appeals to Sherlock Holmes. Mysteries emerge from the bustle of the city outside Baker Street and Holmes, confronted with various kinds of emotional, social, political or fiscal disorder, reasserts order through his ministrations. This oversimplifies the ways in which Doyle treated the particular anxieties of late-century London but it accurately describes the experience of the story from the point of view of the client. In his seminal study of the genre, *Form and Ideology in Crime Fiction* (1980), Stephen Knight observes that Holmes's character is distinguished from his literary-detective forebears by an involvement in the world around him as well as an investment in the emotional and psychological well-being of his clients and their worldview. To client-characters such as Jabez Wilson, Mary Sutherland and Victor Hatherley, Holmes is a combination of accountant, confessor and psychoanalyst. His intellect is a fantastic impossibility that synthesizes unknowable facts from contingent data that in no way corresponds to the real world. One may like to pretend that it is attainable by ordinary readers but it is simply not the case. The clients' *frisson* of excitement when Holmes's attention becomes focused upon their otherwise dull lives for a brief time with violent intensity is not difficult to imagine. The otherwise unremarkable and quotidian life of Mary Sutherland in 'A Case of Identity', for example, is interrupted by the bizarre disappearance of her fiancé and she is suddenly made the subject of Holmes's analysis. She responds by 'g[iving] a violent start [...] with fear and astonishment upon her broad, good-humoured face'. This sensation of intermixed thrill and unease that these characters find when Holmes takes an interest in them is repeated across the canon and continually reinforces the sense of Holmes as an agent capable of resolving criminal threats, financial imbalances, romantic misappropriations and, as Knight characterizes it, other 'middle class worries.'

These characterial and narrative features combined with the nostalgic period-setting and the incipient commodification of the Holmes brand in popular culture to produce what Ed Wiltse has christened a headily 'addictive circuit of author, character, marketplace and reader'.

With a legion of readers sufficiently addicted to this brew, it is little surprise that

Sherlock Holmes, Fan Culture and Fan Letters
Jonathan Cranfield

Fig. 3: Sidney Paget, 'Sherlock Holmes Welcomed Her'. Taken from Arthur Conan Doyle, 'A Case of Identity'. The Strand Magazine 2 (July, 1891), pp. 248–259 (p. 249).

Conan Doyle's attempt to end the Holmes stories in 1893 caused significant withdrawal symptoms. This grief was expressed, tellingly, through a barrage of fan letters which asserted both the truth of Wiltse's observation and the extent to which the letter writers felt their own rights of ownership to have been impinged upon. We know that Conan Doyle was assailed by huge numbers of letters from fans that oscillated between emotional bullying and straightforward abuse. Moreover, Russell Miller's biography recalls that an elderly lady swiped at Conan Doyle in the street with her handbag. The Strand's sister publication Tit-Bits addressed the public in the following terms:

> [L]ike hundreds of correspondents, we feel as if we have lost an old friend whom we could ill spare. Mr Doyle's feeling was that he did not desire Sherlock to outstay his welcome and that the public had had enough of him. This is not our opinion, nor is it the opinion of the public; but it is, we regret to say, Mr Doyle's.

This relationship between the reading public, media platforms and author presaged what Henry Jenkins would later influentially term 'convergence culture' or the cultural forms that emerge when 'old and new media companies try to imagine the future of the entertainment industry'. Doyle's literary and artistic decision to do away with Holmes was eventually subordinated to the exigencies of the new popular literary magazines of which The Strand was only the most popular. Substitute the present potency of Twitter and the prominence of online messageboards for fan letters and the Baker Street Journal and it is perhaps unsurprising that the author suddenly found himself attacked for his retreat from the stories. Conan Doyle was no longer in complete control of a creation whose fictional environs had grown exponentially through the auspices of commodification and marketization. The Conan Doyle archives at Toronto Reference Library, the University of Minnesota and Portsmouth Public Library all contain astonishingly varied catalogues of fan material, both authorized and bootlegged, which had already begun to flood the market by 1893. When fans could already live in a world of Sherlockiana, who was Conan Doyle to pull the plug?

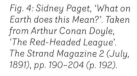

Fig. 4: Sidney Paget, 'What on Earth does this Mean?'. Taken from Arthur Conan Doyle, 'The Red-Headed League'. The Strand Magazine 2 (July, 1891), pp. 190–204 (p. 192).

The fact that Doyle came to have such a real, resentful relationship to his creation is commonly remarked upon. Andrew Lycett notes that in one of Doyle's diaries for 1893, the entry for December simply read '[k]illed Holmes.' In a letter to his mother in April 1893 he said 'I am in the middle of the last Holmes story, after which the gentleman vanishes, never to reappear. I am weary of his name.' These comments seem to reproduce a resentful inversion of the hopeful inquiries of the fan letters, a desperation for the question 'are you real' to receive a firmly negative response; Holmes had indeed become far too real for his liking. The financial incentives offered by Greenhough Smith for further Holmes instalments increased until 1901 brought *The Hound of the Baskervilles*. The rabid public response to the serialized novel prompted *The Strand*'s highest ever domestic distribution and the issues went to seven printings, more than any edition before or after. When, in 1903, Conan Doyle resignedly accepted obscene financial terms from the American *Collier's Magazine* for the Return of Sherlock Holmes series, he was acquiescing to the economic and cultural power of fandom. Whilst whim or fancy may have brought Conan Doyle back to character at some later point, the resuscitation and continuation of the stories was a collective act of will on the part of Holmes fans, manifested by the clear financial windfall that they promised.

One of the most striking aspects of early Sherlock Holmes fan culture was that it established a basic pattern for the ways in which later phenomena would function in the future. When considering the voluminous material resources that are available for fans of products as varied as Star Trek, Disney films, Harry Potter or Game of Thrones (as Henry Jenkins does in his 2013 book *Textual Poachers*) we can trace their faux-seriousness, pretentions to encyclopaedic compilation, and the establishment of a shared, participatory discourse in the early endeavours of Sherlockians. The technology and material cultures that have grown up around these more recent phenomena can also be seen as expedited refinements of those that facilitated Sherlockian fandom over a century ago. Later in life, Conan Doyle was able to acknowledge the 'flattering demand' that had revived Holmes as well as to discover genuine pleasure in allowing others to write their own contributions to the Holmes mythology. His often-reported telegram to William Gillette, upon granting the actor the right to produce his own Sherlock Holmes play, stated 'you may marry him, murder him or do anything you like to him.' Whilst he collaborated directly in some rewritings and watched others from a disdainful distance, he seemed more at peace in acknowledging a kind of diffused ownership of the character and his world. Whilst assuring his copyright and trademarking claims over the character, he developed an attitude that we might anachronistically term 'open-source'. One can easily imagine him observing a project such as Laurie R. King and Leslie Klinger's *A Study in Sherlock* (2011) with benign equanimity. The volume was a collection where numerous high-profile genre-writers including Neil Gaiman and Lee Child offered their own Sherlock Holmes stories.

In the very recent past, these trends have been augmented by the advent of the age of online fanfiction where, according to Busse and Hellekson, 'community-centred creation' can be facilitated electronically amongst disparate groups of people from far-flung corners of the globe. The author's fictional creation becomes a freeform generator of new narratives online where the copyright wrangling of the Conan Doyle Estate has less direct impact. This has had the effect of finally and conclusively legitimizing the worldview of the obsessive writer of fan letters. Their attitude, denigrated and de-

Sherlock Holmes, Fan Culture and Fan Letters
Jonathan Cranfield

rided a century ago, has become a new cultural reality. Instead of broadcasting plaintive appeals into the postal service in hopes of a positive response, they can become fully invested participants and co-creators through direct communication with like-minded fans; no author need apply. ●

~~~~~~~~~~

GO FURTHER

Books

Textual Poachers: Television Fans and Participatory Culture
Henry Jenkins
(London: Routledge, 2013)

A Study in Sherlock: Stories Inspired by the Holmes Canon
Laurie R. King and Leslie Klinger (eds)
(New York: Bantam, 2011)

Byromania and the Birth of Celebrity Culture
Ghislaine McDayter
(New York: State University of New York Press, 2009)

The New Finding Sherlock's London
Thomas Bruce Wheeler
(Bloomington: iUniverse, 2009)

The Adventures of Arthur Conan Doyle
Russell Miller
(London: Harvill Secker, 2008)

Conan Doyle: The Man Who Created Sherlock Holmes
Andrew Lycett
(London: Weidenfeld & Nicolson, 2007)

Fan Fiction and Fan Communities in the Age of the Internet: New Essays
Kristina Busse and Karen Hellekson (eds)
(Jefferson: McFarlane, 2006)

Convergence Culture: Where Old and New Media Collide
Henry Jenkins

(London: New York University Press, 2006)

Fan Cultures
Matt Hills
(London: Routledge, 2002)

Conan Doyle
Michael Coren
(London: Bloomsbury, 1995)

Ventriloquized Bodies: Narratives of Hysteria in Nineteenth-Century France
Janet Beizer
(Ithaca: Cornell University Press, 1994)

Sherlock Holmes: The Complete Novels and Stories, Volumes I and II
Arthur Conan Doyle
(New York: Bantam, 1986)

Letters to Sherlock Holmes
Richard Lancelyn Green (ed.)
(Harmondsworth: Penguin, 1985)

Form and Ideology in Crime Fiction
Stephen Knight
(Basingstoke: MacMillan, 1980)

Extracts/Essays/Articles

'The Strange Case of the Scientist who Believed in Fairies'
Andrew Lycett
In Sabine Vanacker and Catherine Wynne (eds). *Sherlock Holmes and Conan Doyle: Multimedia Afterlives* (Basingstoke: Palgrave MacMillan, 2013), pp. 140–54.

'Modernity, Disenchantment, and the Ironic Imagination'
Michael Saler
In *Philosophy and Literature*. 28: 1 (2004), pp. 137–49.

'The Social Psychology of World Religions'
Max Weber
In *From Max Weber: Essays in Sociology* (London: Routledge, 2004), pp. 267–301.

Sherlock Holmes, Fan Culture and Fan Letters
Jonathan Cranfield

'On the Fetish-Character in Music'
Theodor Adorno
In Richard Leppert (ed.). *Essays on Music* (Berkeley: University of California Press, 2003), pp. 288–317.

'"Clap if you believe in Sherlock Holmes": Mass Culture and the Re-Enchantment of Modernity, c.1890–c.1940'
Michael Saler
In *The Historical Journal*. 46: 3 (2003), pp. 599–622.

'"So Constant an Expectation": Sherlock Holmes and Seriality'
Ed Wiltse
In *Narrative*. 6: 2 (1998), pp. 105–22.

'Studies in the Literature of Sherlock Holmes'
Ronald A. Knox
In *Blackfriars*. 1: 3 (1920), pp. 154–72.

'COME, WATSON, COME!'
HE [HOLMES] CRIED.
'THE GAME IS AFOOT.
NOT A WORD!
INTO YOUR CLOTHES
AND COME!'

'THE ABBEY GRANGE'

Fan Appreciation no.3
The Team behind *The Young Sherlock Holmes Adventures*

Interview by Tom Ue

The following interview with the creative team behind the graphic novel *The Young Sherlock Holmes Adventures* (2010) investigates its creative process, gives an overview of the project, explores what it is like to work in Holmes's home in London, and delves into the comic's visual style. It gives attention to the clues that one may have missed while reading the graphic novel and looks ahead at the series' future. As its title suggests, *The Young Sherlock Holmes Adventures* explores the early days of the hero and his schoolmate James Moriarty. The characters and their creators, as this interview will show, have the opportunities either to follow Conan Doyle's story or create a new one.

Tom Ue: *First off, congratulations on* The Young Sherlock Holmes Adventures! *This first book is an excellent start to what promises to be an engaging and extremely thoughtful series. What moved you to write about young Sherlock?*

Owen Jollands (OJ): *TYSHA* was in development when I graduated the first Masterclass course with Huw-J, and, having been suitably impressed with my colouring and my commitment, Huw-J offered me the position.

Huw-J Davies (HD): I was always fascinated by Basil Rathbone's Holmes and loved the Sir Arthur Conan Doyle originals.

TU: *Recent years have brought a number of different stories about young Sherlock including Andrew Lane's and Shane Peacock's series. Have they affected your thinking about this character? How so?*

OJ: Although I am a huge fan of Sir Arthur Conan Doyle's original works I have steered clear of any further developments on the *TYSHA* front. I think as a studio we all want our ideas to be fresh and as original as possible, which is helped along by the Steampunk setting.

HD: I have purposely avoided reading them. I don't really like being influenced by something so close to the project I am working on.
For example, I am writing an origin for the twin Arthurian swords, so I avoided all films and fantasy books related to that subject. I want the end product to be drawn from the source material so, with the swords project as with Holmes, I look more to the root of the stories, including the historical and social influences of the time.
The nearest to anything new I have looked at has been, of course,

Fan Appreciation no.3
the Team behind *The Young Sherlock Holmes Adventures*

Downey Jr.'s portrayal and the wonderful Moffat's BBC version.
Jane Straw (JS): From a design perspective, I read the original Conan Doyle book but that was years ago! And even working on *TYSHA* I didn't read other takes. So no they didn't affect my thinking of the character. I think more than anything our Sherlock Holmes inherited his character from Huw-J's thumbnails which had a life of their own and was fun to interpret into drawing.

TU: *Do you feel pressured that yours is one of the first comic book versions of a young Sherlock Holmes?*
HD: Lots ha ha.
JS: No. The only pressure was trying to follow in a style already set by another artist. After a while, I realized that I couldn't do it and I had to do my own thing. I think that's when the art in the book improved and became consistent. Unfortunately, it was too late to go back and change some things.
OJ: Initially, the pressure I felt on this book was towards Huw-J and meeting his standards and to Jane to do justice to her line work. Beyond this I think that there is a pressure also to do justice to the characters involved. Not necessarily to turn them into clones of the ACD personalities but certainly to retain the core essence of each character and to portray them to the very best of our abilities.

TU: *Why set your series in Steampunk London?*
OJ: Steampunk London opens up a lot of new options for us and allows us to pick and choose the history that we integrate and that which we amend for our own purposes. Visually the Steampunk idea is very appealing as well and as the universe develops we are really looking to build on this.

TU: *What do you see as the enduring appeals of Steampunk and of London?*
HD: What could have been had Babbage been given the opportunity to really shine, where would the Empire be, and how would the human condition have been affected? The last 30 years have seen more technological progress than the whole of written history put together and the growth rate is almost geometric, if this had happened back then …
OJ: London is one of the best known cities in the world. It is packed full of history both all of its own and from around the globe. There are many famous landmarks and a lot of evocative design. The city has grown organically over the centuries as well rather than being planned from the get go and structured in the more sensible block structures of other famous

cities such as New York.

The Steampunk lets us ask what if, and it lets us take a time not too far removed from our own and play with technology, architecture, fashion and even the attitudes of the people. I think it's a 'New Frontier' ideology which holds a great deal of appeal to us as a race.

TU: *Has working in London impacted your work? How so?*
HD: It's dirty, smelly and uncomfortable. It's challenging, and challenges always affect the way you look at life and how you relate what you experience to storytelling and to writing.
OJ: Working in London has its ups and downs. It's difficult as a fledgling studio as you have a very expensive city to navigate with many stresses that can pile in on top of you.

On the other hand, there is so much reference to draw on from museums, the parks and even the streets and tube.

TU: *The Victorian period ends with the death of Queen Victoria in 1901. Why set your story in 1905?*
HD: SHE DIDN'T DIE! In our story, her life was prolonged but that's a story

Fan Appreciation no.3
the Team behind *The Young Sherlock Holmes Adventures*

that we are bringing out in Issue 4.

OJ: Huw-J is the great story planner and is always thinking ahead on the plot side of things. As I said earlier, the Steampunk setting allows us the freedom to play with the history and follow the what-ifs that we want to explore.

TU: *Sherlock makes quite a distinctive first entrance: he is decked in goggles and riding a motorcycle. Tell us about designing Sherlock.*

HD: Again, it was necessary to create a Sherlock that was true to the source material but has a very unique 'Hayena verse' feel to him. I outlined the characters' parameters, did some sketches of how I felt he should look, showed what I wanted … then handed him over to Yan and Jane. They then worked their magic, and then after a little tweak here and there Jane was given free rein to do her thing.

JS: I was stepping into someone else's shoes: Yan had already done most of the design work so I had simply to follow. I still had to make changes to Yan's design though and he had not designed Malachi or the London Vampire yet (despite constantly asking!).

With all the characters, the design is based on the personality. I always imagine Mal coming from a well-to-do – almost aristocratic – family but wanting to be perceived as 'cool' by hanging round with Sherlock and James. So while the other two go around with their collars up and their tie loose, Mal is proper and primed and trying to fit in.

Being in Steampunk, I had to think of ways of turning the ordinary into interesting stuff. Like the clock on the wall in their room. I hope to take the Steampunk a little further in the next book but still in keeping with the first.

The motorcycle was fun! I managed to prove a penny-cycle Steampunk bike could be done. When I saw Yan's original bike, I kept wondering why the front tyre was 'slightly bigger' and he said it was based on the Penny-cycle. It didn't work because the wheel wasn't significantly bigger so it just looked like an ordinary bike with a wrong wheel on.

Huw-J said I should redesign it, so I said how about a full-on penny-cycle? He said it wouldn't work (in terms of mechanics and physics) but I sent through a sketch and he pretty much said hell yeah!

OJ: Colour-wise, I found it all came very naturally – so much so that my choices almost tone-for-tone matched Yan's original concepts completely independent of each other.

TU: *Why put Sherlock, James and John in the Long Hall School for Boys?*

OJ: We wanted a strong 'base' that was quite versatile and the boarding school fits this requirement for a large number of authors.

TU: *221B Baker Street is translated into a spacious college room, that is numbered 212B, and that is shared by Sherlock, James, Mal and, eventually, Watson. Do you see this change as having a different effect on the relationship between the characters?*
HD: Completely. It forces camaraderie, tension stress, and plays a pivotal role in the relational dynamics of the characters, especially with the inclusion of sexual dynamics via the female cast member.
OJ: We have big plans for the relationships between Holmes, James and Watson – suffice to say again that we are trying to give the whole world our own feel but that we also want everything that happens to happen for a reason.

TU: *Latin is integrated very skilfully through the translation exercise that the boys do at school and the message in blood on the wall. In* A Study in Scarlet (1887), *Watson has claimed that Sherlock has no knowledge of literature despite his immense knowledge of sensational literature. How*

Fan Appreciation no.3
the Team behind *The Young Sherlock Holmes Adventures*

relevant do you see an education in Latin?
OJ: Within the nature of the Steampunk universe that we are crafting and, I believe, within our own modern world, Latin retains a relevance for several reasons. I think that, emotionally, there is a romantic attachment to the language and the feeling of history that comes with it.
There is a power to the language as well which stems from its place as a foundation to our more modern dialects and its association with powerful people and places such as the Roman Empire, kings and queens of old and the Catholic Church.
HD: It's a basis for a lot of our current dialogue and it is often overlooked. I think it has more value than it is given credit for.

TU: *Why make James into, what seems like, Sherlock's closest ally?*
HD: Because your closest friends can hurt you far more than an obvious enemy. Holmes has a lot of lessons to learn along the way to becoming a great detective and being hurt is one of those lessons.
OJ: We wanted the events of the universe to hold relevance and to happen for a reason. Huw-J wouldn't want me to give much more away here though.

TU: *At this stage in the story, it's unclear if James will follow his father Professor Moriarty's footsteps and become Sherlock's nemesis or if James will go on being Sherlock's sidekick. Indeed, James's decision to have his father buried in a pauper's grave suggests the latter. Is James's ambiguous position here deliberate?*
HD: That would be giving away too much ... but let me just say that if things progress as planned the character will indeed change. Remember nothing is clear cut and the motives for evil can sometimes start in an attempt to do good.

TU: *Mal is a fascinating character not least of all because he comes in with a tray of teacakes after James chides Sherlock for his insensitivity about James's mother's murder. Most of what Mal says is ignored by his colleagues. This minor character quickly becomes central to the story. Why make him one of the foci?*
HD: Because it was unexpected and lay the foundation for the dynamics of the characters' interactions.
OJ: One of Huw-J's favourite devices is to work in subtlety, something that I think lends itself well to Sherlock. There are hints throughout the story that Mal is perhaps more important than he at first seems to be. Whether they pick this up and unravel the mystery or are surprised by the

end doesn't matter, it just means different readers will have different experiences.

TU: *The original Sherlock Holmes canon has been read as being strongly masculine. Is the inclusion of Chetan, the daughter of a Professor Mishra and a sidekick, a deliberate move against such readings?*
HD: Yes. Simply put there needed to be a feminine strong character to pull away from the obvious devices of the original language
OJ: Chetan has several roles but one of the elements Hayena is trying to develop is that of strong, relevant female characters. Sara and Jane will keep us on track here I'm sure but we want to make sure that as the stories develop no one gets left out.

TU: *In a pivotal moment in the story – when Sherlock follows Chetan around London – you move from dialogue to third-person narration. This change distances the reader and enables you, eventually, to cut back and forth between Chetan dancing and the matron accosting the – to avoid spoilers – murderer as s/he approaches Mal. Tell us about this narrative change, and give us a glimpse of what happened behind the scenes of the three pages with all the cross-cutting.*
HD: This was a deliberate move to create mood and texture to the story while allowing the mystery of Mal's involvement to remain hidden until the right moment. A good storyteller never gives away everything instantly but rather unfolds organically and with the right timing the tapestry that he weaves.
OJ: For me, this was one of the most fun elements of the story to colour. I experimented with a few options, particularly when it came to Chetan's dance scene. I tried a few panels with the crowd watching included, but settled on just the focus of Chetan herself with the heat and light responding to her movements.
   I was trying to contrast the warmth of the atmosphere and moment in the temple with that of the coldness of the school halls and the murder.
I think that the cross-cutting between the two allowed us to show a deeper duality within life as well and to demonstrate that principle of your own greatest moment also being the very worst for someone else.

TU: *Chetan is connected again and again to Felix Leiter, who introduces himself to Sherlock, and who appears many times throughout the book. Can you tell us more about this character and their connection?*
HD: To be honest, if I give this away, I am giving away the plot of the sec-

Fan Appreciation no.3
the Team behind *The Young Sherlock Holmes Adventures*

ond book and that's not going to happen. Let's just say that the clues are there.

OJ: Felix is one of a host of secondary characters that is going to help us tie the disparate stories together and bring the events of one character's story into another's. Huw-J plays his cards close to his chest though, so I can't tell you much more suffice to say that his role will become clearer as the stories progress.

TU: *Like Conan Doyle's stories,* The Young Sherlock Holmes Adventures *repeatedly gestures towards larger international relations, as evidenced by both Professor Mishra's return from India and the Indian Quarters in London. Tell us more about this international focus.*

HD: Again book two and the idea of Victoria still being monarch play heavily on this. But this is the second book so spoilers are going to be a no-no.

OJ: Part of the thrill of building a universe is in the variety that you can explore. To not make use of a global landscape would be, in my opinion, very limiting. Global events give you much more scope and freedom and when you talk about the Empire as we have it doesn't mean anything unless you set that within the bigger global landscape.

TU: *Recent criticism about Conan Doyle's short stories has revealed how ambivalent they are about the relationship between England and the wider world. Have these conversations informed your thinking about the story?*

HD: Not really there is a clear distinction in the universe where our characters are playing out. The Empire still rules with an iron fist.

TU: *Can you tell us more about the 'Revolutions Plans' to which Felix refers? Can you give us a sneak-peek of what's in store for Sherlock?*

OJ: Huw-J won't let me.

HD: That last comment about empire is probably my biggest hint to this.

TU: *One of the most impressive things about* The Young Sherlock Holmes Adventures *is its abundance in details. James has a poster of Harriet Beecher Stowe's immensely popular novel* Uncle Tom's Cabin (1852) *or one of its adaptations on his wall. Tell us a bit about the things that we might not notice in a first reading.*

HD: Houdini didn't give away his tricks! There will always be layers of clues for future events laid into the stories along with little nods to the characters roots. These we layer visually and verbally. But sometimes it's just us having fun and giving you more things to draw you into the world and story.

After all, we want to immerse you into the world and enjoy the story. We want you to care about the characters not just read and drop the book by the side of the loo. We want these books on your shelves for you and your friends to read as well as your kids. I'm all about the kids reading these stories and getting inspired to read the originals

OJ: There are many Easter Eggs scattered around *TYSHA* book. Some of these are scripted such as the Felix Leiter character and others are drawn, but as the colourist and letterist I really got to let loose and throw in lots of little treats.

The wanted poster from the back gallery makes several appearances in the story, as do references to two other graphic novels from Markosia – Huw-J's *Freeman* and *Dark Mists*. I've even slipped in a missing notice for my own cat (fictional – the notice, not the cat) and several references from the Sherlock Holmes and The Lost World books.

You may even be able to gather a couple of hints about the next book's storyline from some of the sketch gallery pages at the back. Though I'm not letting you know which ones.

And of course as this is my first book and my girlfriend was so supportive, she's featured in my notes page holding our cat and wearing a very funky hat.

JS: The cameo by Phileas Fogg. But I'm not telling where! All credit to Owen though. He seems to have been on a roll! There are some personal artworks from my portfolio dotted around too, which he slipped in the main school hall along with a personal photo of his. Owen also put in a script commending the person if they were able to read it at all! You need a magnifying glass but I don't know if even that will work.

TU: *Thank you so much for your time and best wishes with this exciting new series!* . ●

GO FURTHER

Books

The Young Sherlock Holmes Adventures
Huw-J Davies, Owen Jollands and Jane Straw
(London: Markosia, 2010)

Chapter
5

Sherlock Holmes in the Twenty-second Century: Rebranding Holmes for a Child Audience

Noel Brown

→ Endlessly imitated, parodied and pastiched, Sherlock Holmes's multifaceted appeal can be gauged by the several attempts to adapt the stories – and, perhaps more centrally, the rationalist imperative at their core – for young audiences. Screen adaptations of Conan Doyle's stories intended chiefly for children and families have fared variably. They include Granada Television's short-lived live-action miniseries *Young Sherlock* (1982); Steven Spielberg's sprightly but underperforming blockbuster *Young Sherlock Holmes* (Barry Levinson, 1985); Australian Company Burbank Films's comparatively dreary animated retellings of Conan Doyle's four Holmes novels (1983), starring an extraordinarily bored-sounding Peter O'Toole; the Japanese anime series *Sherlock Hound* (1984–85), co-directed by Studio Ghibli luminary Hayao Miyazaki, which was dubbed into English and has gained a cult following; and Disney's often-overlooked 1986 feature animation *The Great Mouse Detective*, which anthropomorphically riffs on the premise.

Fig. 1: The reimagined Baker Street Irregulars

All of these productions trade on the multimedia brand potential of Sherlock Holmes. Holmes is both a universally-recognized literary figure and a cult phenomenon and it is this pre-existing global consumer-base, as well as the inherent appeal of the stories and their central figure, which motivate screen adaptations of this kind. There may be a vague, essentially well-meaning but uncoordinated desire to stimulate children's interest in the literary source material, but it should be emphasized that the above productions are commercial initiatives, and thus primarily predicated on escapist, rather than didactic, modes of narrative. Perhaps the most interesting retelling of Sherlock Holmes for children – because it was explicitly promoted as educational as well as entertaining – is the animated series *Sherlock Holmes in the 22nd Century* (Sandy Ross, 1999–2001), a British (Scottish Television) and North American (DiC Entertainment) co-production, broadcasted in Britain by ITV, and in the United States by Fox.

Sherlock Holmes in the 22nd Century spanned 26 episodes, ultimately split into two series, after which the show was not renewed. Its Anglo-American origins are perceptible from its diverse formal influences, which splice the characteristic Victoriana of the Conan Doyle stories with a more contemporary visual aesthetic that draws on the iconography of cyberpunk and steampunk. The basic premise is that the preserved body of Sherlock Holmes is resuscitated in early-twenty-second-century 'New London' by the New Scotland Yard detective, Inspector Beth Lestrade (voiced by Akiko Morison). Once resuscitated, Holmes is asked to help combat a complex new crime wave, ultimately revealed to have been initiated by a similarly-revived Moriarty (Richard Newman). Here rendered as a younger (twenty-something), more gregarious character (voiced by Canadian Jason Gray-Stanford), Holmes is aided by a New Scotland Yard-operated robot (John Payne), who downloads Dr Watson's diaries and, augmented with a high-tech face mask, appropriates his identity. According to a production diary, the series was intended to cater to children between the ages of 6 and 11. The concept of an animated Sherlock Holmes series aimed at children was felt by both production partners to 'appeal to both the American and UK markets' and 'the combination of the Sherlock Holmes recogni-

Sherlock Holmes in the Twenty-second Century:
Rebranding Holmes for a Child Audience
Noel Brown

tion factor and the mystery/sci-fi aspect of the series' was hyperbolically pitched as constituting 'an entirely new genre for animation'.

This chapter is primarily concerned with the strategies employed by the show's producers to rebrand Conan Doyle's adult-orientated Sherlock Holmes stories as a children's show possessing pedagogic as well as narrative and aesthetic appeal. We must begin by noting that, although Holmes exhibits certain traits clearly undesirable from an instructional perspective (including violence, narcissism, misogyny and a predilection for substance abuse), he also exemplifies a man of reason, embodying rationalism, self-control, and other Enlightenment values still valorized as aspirational hallmarks of civilization. To this extent, the central premises of Conan Doyle's stories are perceptibly translatable to juvenile audiences, although not without modification. Certain reconfigurations (discussed below in greater depth) are highly suggestive: (1) the clear attempts to position Holmes as an identification figure and displace the aloofness hitherto regarded as intrinsic to his appeal while simultaneously democratizing his science of deduction; (2) the reconfiguration of the Baker Street Irregulars, originally street urchins occupying a marginal position in the Holmes pantheon, as leading characters; (3) the basic fidelity to the original stories, each episode being loosely based on a Conan Doyle story and with similarly loose continuity between individual instalments, as with some of *The Strand Magazine* stories[1]; (4) the futuristic, sci-fi setting, drawing on the established popularity of science fiction and fantasy among young audiences; and (5) the brief (twenty minutes, without adverts) running time, in accordance with the commonly-held requirements of most children for shorter forms of entertainment.

The Children's Television Act

Although primarily a commercial concern, *Sherlock Holmes in the 22nd Century* was made according to the prescripts of the Children's Television Act (1990; amended 1996) which mandated that television broadcasters in the United States show a minimum of three hours of 'educational'/'informational' content per week – a requirement enforced by the Federal Communications Commission (FCC). The key requirements of the Act include: serving the educational and informational needs of children aged 16 and under as a significant purpose; the programme being aired between the hours of 7.00 a.m. and 10.00 p.m. with a major broadcaster; the programme being a regularly-scheduled weekly programme; the programme being at least thirty minutes in length (with adverts); and the target child audience/age group being provided by the distributor. *Sherlock Holmes in the 22nd Century* – as with many children's television shows for US consumption – was manufactured explicitly to conform to these regulations.

An educational consultant was employed to ensure its pedagogic suitability, and the website of the show's current distributor, Cookie Jar Entertainment (successor to the now-defunct DiC) emphasizes its educative potential. The corresponding sales pitch on the *CJar.biz* website is worth repeating in its entirety:

Sherlock Holmes' timely return offers an ideal device for engaging and entertaining young viewers while building invaluable problem-solving and information management skills; and modelling the pro-social values and behaviours associated with enduring friendships and effective teamwork.

We want viewers to be so caught up in the characters' relationships and adventures and so drawn by Holmes' passion for problem solving, for teamwork and healthy competition, for the thrill of the chase, the excitement of denouement, and the deep satisfaction of a case well-solved – that they naturally adopt positive attitudes and behaviours.

In addition, on the website each of the 26 episodes has a one-line summary of its 'educational focus'. For instance, the opening episode, 'The Rise and Fall of Sherlock Holmes', is said to reinforce the value of 'flexib[ility] when problem solving' and 'being able to change a theory when the validated facts don't fit'. 'The Hound of the Baskervilles' (Series 1, Episode 3), meanwhile, underlined that 'it is fool-

Figs. 2&3: The 22nd Century 'New London' cityscape

ish to hold on to a belief (or superstition) when evidence contradicts it'; 'The Adventure of the Empty House' (Series 1, Episode 5), asserted that 'no matter how bad things look, it's important to handle your emotions and not fall apart; strong emotions can interfere with logical thinking' and 'The Five Orange Pips' (Series 1, Episode 15) provided 'a lesson against bigotry and racial intolerance'.

Of course, critical perspective demands that we treat these inferred attributes with some scepticism; some of the asserted educational messages are so nebulous that one doubts their intent. Nevertheless, it is true that several episodes strongly foreground rationalistic and/or humanistic themes. Holmes's quickly-wearing catchphrase, 'eyes and brains', constitutes a shorthand and memorable affirmation of rational observation over impressionistic assumption. There are more specific examples of the series' 'right-on' approach. In a festive Christmas episode, 'The Adventure of the Blue Carbuncle' (Series 1, Episode 13), Holmes is an arbiter of anti-commercialization, specifically what he perceives as the commodification of Christmas. He observes, 'I never realized how much I enjoyed Victorian Christmases until I experienced a modern one' and insisting – with a forceful and romanticizing anti-materialism at odds with the decadent Holmes presented by Conan Doyle – that 'In my day, Christmas was about spending time with family and friends [...] Christmas should be more about enjoying what you have, not what

Sherlock Holmes in the Twenty-second Century:
Rebranding Holmes for a Child Audience
Noel Brown

you get'. 'The Five Orange Pips', meanwhile, carries racial and anti-colonial subtexts in Doctor Watson's harsh treatment from 'anti-techs' – an aristocratic, patrician collective zealously opposed to mechanization and to whom the late-Victorian-era way of life is defiantly upheld. One such character laments, 'Little by little, we are losing our humanity to these machines.' Suggestively, a young boy raised by his anti-tech father to despise robots ultimately sees the error of his ways after the kindly, robotic Doctor Watson saves his father's life.

In most episodes, however, these didactic impulses are subsumed by a more escapist trajectory, and didacticism is localized to the representation of Holmes. Although his infallibility is subsequently reaffirmed at all junctures, in the opening episodes, a discomfited Holmes initially has to overcome his prejudices towards a female superior and a robot companion. By the end of the second episode, 'The Crime Machine', he has come to accept both, but only after a semi-comic exchange in which Lestrade asserts that Holmes will be working under her:

Holmes: You? Balderdash! What sort of a world has this become?
Lestrade: A better one – for women.
Holmes: And men?
Watson: That rather depends on the man, wouldn't you say?

Thus, gender and racial equality (the latter allegorically through Watson's emerging status as a liberated slave/subordinate) are quickly affirmed. In other episodes, Holmes explicitly draws moral lessons. For instance, in 'The Adventure of the Beryl Board' (Series 2, Episode 7), a story in which a wealthy tycoon wrongly suspects his son of betrayal and penitently asks for forgiveness at the end, Holmes observes, 'Take heed, Watson. Even if children have made mistakes in the past, they still need to be listened to and respected […] Along with love, forgiveness is what keeps a family together – in this age, or any other.' Dialogue such as this help establish the series' relevance – and that of the moral messages therein – to contemporary audiences, emphasizing the desirable continuities (the pronounced importance of the family) while simultaneously eliding ostensibly child-unfriendly points of tension, such as Victorian-era colonialism and oppression of women. In such scenes, the benignly relatable Watson, who appears largely unable to form judgements of his own independent of Holmes's influence, functions as an avatar for the presumably similarly apolitical child audience.

A twenty-second-century Sherlock Holmes

Inevitably, the series presents a highly populist (and marketable) image of Holmes which draws on a kind of folk memory of the detective and what he represents. This much may be gauged from the title sequence, which presents a montage of representative clips from the show, sequentially presenting (1) the famous Sherlock Holmes silhouette –

Figs. 4: The robotic Dr. Watson

Figs. 5: The reanimated Holmes.

suggestively without his unhealthy, non-PC pipe; (2) a shot of a hover-car bursting out of the silhouette into the bustling metropolis of nocturnal New London; (3) a short clip of Holmes and Moriarty locked in combat at Reichenbach Falls, framed by a futuristic TV screen; (4) Lestrade bringing Holmes back to life; (5) a newly-revived and youthful Holmes engaging with Watson, interspersed with further shots of the darkened city; (6) Moriarty returning to life and cackling maniacally; and (7) various sequences of Holmes and Watson in peril, interspersed with yet more clips of the metropolis. The sequence ends by returning to the still of Holmes's silhouette, overlaid with his voice characteristically (but erroneously, as the phrase never appeared in any of Conan Doyle's adventures) intoning, 'Elementary, my dear Watson.' The title sequence gives a very quick summary of the premise of the series, whilst communicating certain key information regarding its approach; it is futuristic and action-packed, but clearly draws on certain inherited conventions: Holmes's basic appearance and ethos, the presence of Watson, the antagonistic role of Moriarty, etc.[2] The electronic, vaguely punkish music seems designed to convey a sense of urgency and edginess, while its only lyrics – a tiresomely repetitive refrain of 'Sherlock Holmes in the twenty-second century' – drives the point home. Of course, this assertion of 'newness' in the series' postmodern aesthetics serves an important secondary function: disavowing its more traditional (if liberally-inflected) moral overtones. Formal progressiveness and ideological conservatism thus operate dialectically in fulfilment of the series' dual agenda of entertainment and instruction.

This animated Holmes is truly a man for all seasons. Possessed of all of the intellectual and physical attributes of his literary precursor, but also handsome (as Lestrade implies in the opening episode), youthful, cheerful, enthusiastic, collegial, compassionate and empathetic, he has become a hero – and, perhaps more importantly, an avuncular identification figure and role model. As such, the twenty-second century Holmes is much more benign than Conan Doyle's anti-hero. Seemingly clean-living, presumably having dispensed with his cocaine addiction, he also becomes a more liberal figure in his acceptance of female authority figure, and de facto superior, Lestrade, and in his comparatively empathetic relationships with other characters.[3] Although evidently still convinced of his intellectual superiority, his conceit rarely translates as cold aloofness, as in the books – and, indeed, Moffat's and Gatiss's *Sherlock* (BBC, 2010–). While initially he displays irritation at Lestrade's robot masquerading as his deceased friend, very

Sherlock Holmes in the Twenty-second Century:
Rebranding Holmes for a Child Audience
Noel Brown

quickly he comes warmly to accept this imposter as the genuine article. His constant newfound cheerfulness contrasts sharply with his taciturn representations by Conan Doyle, where manic depression or some other mental illness may be inferred from his extended periods of morbid self-absorption. His language, too, has become more conversational, less rigid; it is little more than a parody of formal English – a fact that reflects the trans-Atlantic audience-base as well as primarily juvenile address.[4]

Points may fruitfully be made concerning the role of Sherlock Holmes in this future society. The fictional world presented is a curious hybrid of utopian (deriving from its child-orientated modalities) and dystopian (deriving from its aesthetic influences) creative impulses. The so-called 'crypnotic' programming through which criminal minds are 'cured' of their sociopathic tendencies certainly borders on the kinds of mind control posited by the likes of Huxley, Orwell and Kafka, even if its avowed purpose is benign and its implementation restricted to proven malefactors.[5] Nevertheless, this world appears, if only from its aesthetic invocations, to be a dangerous place, forever shrouded – like the noirish tones of cyberpunk – in darkness and shadows. This future society is also heavily reliant on technology. Predictably, everyone now travels in flying cars but beyond this tokenistic detail there are suggestions of more anxiety-producing overreliance on mechanization. Public law-enforcement is now partially conducted by presumably-incorruptible but emotionless robots (such as Watson who, prior to his reassuring transformation into a near-perfect simulacrum of Holmes's friend, is bureaucratic, untrustworthy and – as the property of New Scotland Yard – is allied to 'those suits upstairs'). A central computer holds all public information and governs power allocation, and it proves, over the course of the series, highly susceptible to hacking. In the context of this future society, which is comprised of a combination of the familiar and unfamiliar, Sherlock Holmes is a stable, knowable, element in a future world of alienating technological intricacy.

From his familiar Inverness cape and deerstalker hat to his well-worn catchphrases which have been thoroughly implanted in the popular consciousness, he serves, perhaps for the first time, as the audience's central identification figure. His intellectual precision – the precision of a supremely-honed human mind, rather than the cold logic of the machine – is leavened by sentiment and emotion, demonstrated throughout in his indulgent acknowledgement of Lestrade's robot as his long-lost friend (whom, he admits in the opening episode, he misses 'more than I care to admit'), his growing regard for Lestrade and his paternalistic relationship with the Baker Street Irregulars – and, by extension, with young audiences. Holmes makes a potentially-dangerous and alien world safe. Perhaps more than any other modern representation, *Sherlock Holmes in the 22nd Century* demonstrates the extent to which its mythology has been reconfigured in the popular imaginary through its various affirmations, retellings and recapitulations.[6]

Fig. 6: Holmes in silhouette in the title sequence

Fig. 7: Moriarty.

Modes of appeal

The Baker Street Irregulars – the gang of street urchins on which Conan Doyle's Holmes occasionally relied for help in cases – fulfil a much more important narrative role in *Sherlock Holmes in the 22nd Century*. As with many other modern children's television shows (and in contrast with pre-1990s orthodoxy), the series presents a group of empowered late-teenagers in the Irregulars. The group are somewhat older than the target audience and hence characters towards whom young viewers may aspire in their autonomy, competence and hipness. In 'The Adventure of the Dancing Men' (Series 1, Episode 11), the Irregulars – dissatisfied with their established roles as gatherers of evidence – request a more active role in the cases, which Holmes, over the objections of Watson and Lestrade (who doubt the youngsters' competency) concedes. With Holmes's guidance, the Irregulars are instrumental in solving the case.

The narratives ascribe to a well-worn formula. Necessarily, given the format, most episodes open in the thick of the action, with a short voice-over by Watson establishing the nature of the case. Invariably, Holmes is one step ahead of his cohorts, with Watson and Lestrade consistently making false assumptions (although Lestrade's kick-ass combat skills frequently extricate Holmes from tight situations). Roughly half of the episodes revolve around a nefarious scheme concocted by Moriarty – the producers seemingly having decided that a recurring villain is necessary to provide continuity for the benefit of the target demographic – with various henchmen, such as the grotesque geneticist Martin Fenwick, providing muscle. Such sub-villains also serve important structural (and, from an audience perspective, emotional) roles. As a recurring arch-villain, Moriarty must remain at liberty at the end of each episode; indeed, several stories end with him apparently cornered, at gunpoint, before he escapes through some sleight-of-hand (one well-worn example is his deployment of a smoke-bomb; in others, he simply runs away). The capture of his underlings therefore brings the story to a structurally-fulfilling climax while still providing a note of suspense – and a hook – for future instalments.

The comfortingly-predictable narrative structure – mirroring that of other children's television shows from *Sesame Street* (Lloyd Morrisett and Joan Ganz Cooney, NET, 1969–) and *Scooby-Doo* (Joe Ruby and Ken Spears, CBS, 1969–) to *The Teletubbies* (Anne Wood and Andrew Davenport, BBC, 1997–2001) – serves to reinforce the essentially affirmative properties of the series. Structure, routine and repetition, supported by equally structuring didactic principles, are primary means through which the show

Sherlock Holmes in the Twenty-second Century:
Rebranding Holmes for a Child Audience
Noel Brown

appeals to young audiences, but also, moreover, can be *seen* to do so, according to the accepted pedagogical standards by which it has to conform. Unusually, from this perspective – though also unavoidably, because of its cancellation due to low ratings – the series ends on something of a cliffhanger, with the ongoing Holmes–Moriarty struggle unresolved. Broadcast in dedicated children's television slots in both the United Kingdom and United States, neither ratings nor awareness were likely to be substantial. Predictably, it has also encountered derision among the Holmes *cognoscenti* for its eccentric premise, although in later years has gained something of a cult audience, belatedly receiving a DVD release in 2012. Whilst little more than a footnote in the annals of Holmes fiction, *Sherlock Holmes in the 22nd Century* is nevertheless notable in its recognition of the enduring appeal of Sherlock Holmes, and of the adaptability of its core tenets for juvenile consumption. ●

Notes
1. The stories are clearly written and produced by people with close knowledge of the property's literary and filmic heritage. For instance, Holmes's and Watson's character animation is clearly modelled on Basil Rathbone and Nigel Bruce, who portrayed the detective and his associate in a phenomenally popular series of live-action films in the 1930s and 1940s.
2. Moriarty only appeared in very few of Conan Doyle's stories, although his centrality in Holmesian law is tightly inscribed in subsequent retellings.
3. To this extent, we see a purging of late-nineteenth-century social prejudices in Holmes of the kind previously identified by Ronald R. Thomas; see 'The Fingerprint of the Foreigner'.
4. In 'The Adventure of the Engineer's Thumb' (Series 2, Episode 3), one such person forcibly objects to having his brain 'scrambled'; with clinical euphemism, Lestrade insists, 'We don't scramble brains. We modify Chromosomal behaviour through science.'
5. *Sherlock Holmes in the 22nd Century* is not the first, or the last, updating of Holmes to a modern setting. The later Basil Rathbone films transpose Holmes to 1940s (i.e. wartime) Britain, while the recent, high-profile BBC update, *Sherlock*, is set in modern, post-millennial London. Two TV movies, CBS's *The Return of Sherlock Holmes* (Kevin Connor, 1987) and Granada Television's *Sherlock Holmes Returns* (Kenneth Johnson, 1993), fancifully involve a cryogenically-suspended Holmes returning to solve modern mysteries.
6. This is in accordance with a seminal 1950s independent film syllogism, cited by Noel Brown, which held that, to appeal to the broadest age demographic, you must 'zero in on the 19-year-old male'.

GO FURTHER

Books

The Hollywood Family Film: A History, from Shirley Temple to Harry Potter
Noel Brown
(London/New York: I.B. Tauris, 2012)

Extracts/Essays/Articles

'The Fingerprint of the Foreigner: Colonising the Criminal Body in 1890s Detective Fiction and Criminal Anthropology'
Ronald R. Thomas
In *ELH*. 61: 3 (1994) [Online], pp. 655–83, http://www.jstor.org/stable/2873339.

Films and Television

Sherlock Holmes in the 22nd Century, Paul Quinn, dir. (U.K., U.S.: DIC Entertainment, STV Productions, 1999-2001).

Online

'MIPCOM Report: Co-production diary: Sherlock Holmes in the 22nd Century'
Ed Kirchdoerffer
Kidscreen. Engaging the Global Children's Entertainment Industry. 1 October 1996, http://kidscreen.com/1996/10/01/17303-19961001/.

'Educational/Informational Compliant Titles from Cookie Jar's Extensive Library – CJar.biz: Sherlock Holmes in the 22nd Century'. *CJar.biz*, http://www.cjar.biz/sherlock_holmes.html.

Fan Appreciation no.4
Scott Beatty, co-author of *Sherlock Holmes: Year One*

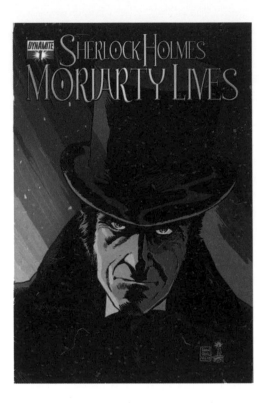

Interview by Tom Ue

The similarities between *The Young Sherlock Holmes Adventures* (Huw-J Davies, Owen Jollands and Jane Straw, 2010) and Scott Beatty's and Daniel Lindro's *Sherlock Holmes: Year One* (2011) are as instructive as their visual differences. Both series tell stories of the young and inexperienced youth who meets Watson for the first time, and speak to recent trends in Holmes's fandom. In the interview below, Beatty looks back at his own experience of Holmes, comments on the influence of contemporary events, and explores his own relations to Holmes's creator, whom he acknowledges through intertextuality.

Tom Ue: *Congratulations on* Sherlock Holmes: Year One! *How did this project begin? What made you turn to Holmes?*
Scott Beatty: Actually, it was Dynamite Entertainment's idea. Head honcho Nick Barucci and Executive Editor Joseph Rybandt approached me about scripting a 'Year One' story with Holmes and Watson. I had co-written a trifecta of Y1 stories at DC Comics involving the Bat-Characters (Robin, Batgirl and Nightwing), so I suppose it was time for me to tackle Sherlock Holmes, certainly an influence on every fictional detective to follow him. Plus, I had written RUSE for a bit over two years at CrossGen Comics. The characters and relationships in that series, set in a Victorian-esque era on a far-flung planet, are very much inspired by Sir Arthur Conan Doyle's work.

TU: *You have worked on many comic books before. In what ways is this experience similar and/or different from your previous work?*
SB: For me, it was a deeper immersion into research than most of my other works. Certain comics' worlds allow for willing suspension of disbelief. With Holmes, I believe the audience is owed a much greater attention to detail and realism (as it applies to nineteenth-century London).

TU: *What do you see as Holmes's enduring appeal?*
SB: Look at the current television landscape. Subtract sitcoms and reality-based offerings and the rest is a panoply of procedural crime dramas, none of which would exist without the deductive sleuthing of Sherlock Holmes and Dr Watson.

TU: *When did your interest in Holmes begin?*
SB: As a kid. Though as far as detectives go, my 'gateway' characters to Sherlock Holmes were Batman (The Dark Knight Detective) and boy sleuth Encyclopedia Brown, who headlined a long-running series of chil-

Fan Appreciation no.4
Scott Beatty, co-author of Sherlock Holmes: Year One

dren's books. After a bit of Holmes name-dropping in stories with the for-mer, I scoured my school library to see what I was missing.

TU: *Representations of Holmes as a younger man are significantly fewer than those of him as a middle-aged one. What made you focus on young Holmes?*
SB: We've all seen Holmes in Point B. But few stories – whether in film, television or prose – focus on Point A. Interestingly, Holmes's motiva-tions are often inscrutable in the stories. I was very much interested in the events that led him to a life consumed by solving mysteries, not to mention Watson's take on it all.

TU: *What are some of the advantages and/or disadvantages of this focus?*
SB: For both, it's continuity. My self-imposed rule from the start was to find a way to make my story fit into Doyle's 'canon' without negating any other story. I wanted *SHYO* to be a part of the long tapestry. When it's all said and done, readers will see that it fits 'between' a few well-remembered and much-loved Holmes adventures without (ideally) negating anything.

TU: *Visually, your series is quite distinctive from other recent interpreta-tions. Do you feel pressured by them?*
SB: For my part, the pressure is mainly being 'realistic' yet retaining the freedom of fiction to open up new worlds, not to mention new stories.

TU: *Although your Holmes is set in the Victorian period, you include in-corporate many pre-Victorian texts and images. What fascinates you about them?*
SB: Let's just say that the central crime in the series, 'The Twelve Caesars', involves a mystery that began many centuries before the Victorian period.

TU: *Shakespeare, for instance, makes many appearances, including a performance of* Julius Caesar *and Holmes's drawing on* Henry IV, Part 2 *when he says: 'Heavy is the head that wears the crown.' Why bring in Shakespeare?*
SB: Shakespeare is England's most celebrated dramatist and he wrote plays that centred upon murders or crimes. I suppose that makes the Bard a fellow mystery writer.

TU: *Has your thinking about Holmes changed during the writing? How so?*
SB: If anything, he's more human to me. Holmes is larger-than-life. He's

Fig. 1: Extracts from Sherlock
Holmes: Moriarty Lives

quite super-heroic in his uncanny ability to deconstruct a mystery and point an accusatory finger at
the one true culprit. I wanted to see what it means
for him to have this power and why he chooses to
use it. He could be anything. He's the smartest guy in the room, yet he
chooses to make his living by plumbing the depths of human depravity.

TU: *This series is dedicated to Arthur Conan Doyle. Did you feel pressured
by his writing? How so?*
SB: I think any writer who takes up the standard of a much-beloved fictional hero owes both gratitude and a sense of responsibility to honour
the work and his creator.

TU: *The short-story form had a profound impact on Conan Doyle's stories,
as did their publication in* The Strand Magazine, *a middle-class-oriented
monthly. Did the form of the comic book affect the mystery story? How so?*
SB: In comics, every issue is a short story and should be treated as such.
But each issue is also a chapter to the larger mystery and should 'scaffold'
into a much more satisfying read when taken as a whole.

Fan Appreciation no.4
Scott Beatty, co-author of Sherlock Holmes: Year One

TU: *You thanked Holmes expert Leslie Klinger at the start of Issues 2–5. In what ways did Leslie help with this project?*
SB: Les was actually on board since the first issue. As an expert on Holmes and Doyle's writings, he provided invaluable feedback on minutiae that was crucial to the story. He's our resident 'fact-checker'.

TU: *Your series opens with a brilliant first line from Watson's perspective – 'I hate mysteries' – and with his examination of Holmes's wounds. Tell us about your decisions behind Holmes's and Watson's first meeting.*
SB: I think it was absolutely necessary that they first met at the scene of a crime, each employed by the London Police in a different capacity. That and Holmes himself would be the mystery that Watson was compelled to solve.

TU: *The scenes of the Battle of Maiwand are beautifully drawn and coloured. Tell us about the writing and drawing of them.*
SB: For me, Watson's history was even more compelling than Holmes's backstory. The good doctor had seen horrors of his own, including service in a distant country that continues to bedevil western powers determined to tame it. Not a judgement, but merely an observation with history as prelude.

Your Watson tells us:
A Jezail bullet adding insult to injury by nicking my subclavian artery after shattering the shoulder bone. I began my commission as assistant surgeon of the army medical department, 66th foot in the Second Afghan War but I ended my military career as a simple soldier doing his level best to stay alive.

This description is much bitterer than Conan Doyle's for Watson:
The campaign brought honours and promotion to many, but for me it had nothing but misfortune and disaster. [...] There [in Maiwand] I was struck on the shoulder by a Jezail bullet, which shattered the bone and grazed the subclavian artery. I should have fallen into the hands of the murderous Ghazis had it not been for the devotion and courage shown by Murray, my orderly.

TU: *Have contemporary views about war affected your thinking? How so?*
SB: I'd prefer to let the words speak for themselves. But as a witness to history unfolding minute-by-minute on cable news, I'm certainly influenced by the conflicts overseas. Watson is reflecting on the events that ended his dreams of being a surgeon. Who wouldn't be bitter at that?

Fig. 2: Extracts from Sherlock
Holmes: Moriarty Lives

TU: *Holmes calls attention to Watson's skills as a storyteller. Do you see Holmes as being privileged with these same qualities?*

SB: Watson embellishes, as all writers do. Holmes is more concerned with empirical facts, not flowery descriptions or other distractions from THE TRUTH.

TU: *How did you approach Holmes's voice to make it different from those of the other characters?*

SB: Holmes has a singular focus. He values information and knowledge above every other pursuit, and that comes through in his voice and characterization.

TU: *In terms of narration, you alternate between Holmes's, Watson's, and third-person perspectives. What do you see as the value of this approach?*

SB: An omniscient voice would know the answer to the mystery. Watson doesn't and Holmes doesn't, and part of the excitement is finding the clues with them in as close to 'real time' as a graphic novelization permits. Detective work is all about DISCOVERY.

Fan Appreciation no.4
Scott Beatty, co-author of Sherlock Holmes: Year One

TU: *Your series is meticulously researched, and it draws on Conan Doyle's writing about Holmes in his younger days, as evidenced, for instance, when Watson tells Holmes: 'I had a most difficult time already convincing Inspector Bratton of your usefulness, despite what I'm told you did to sort out that Musgrave business.' However, 'The Musgrave Ritual' is not a case in which Holmes was clearly defeated. Why have Holmes criticized here?*
SB: Ah, a story for another time! Year Two? Let's just say that Bratton and the police sometimes bristle at having to rely on a young upstart like Sherlock Holmes to sort out the criminality in their bailiwick.

TU: *In many ways, your Watson is a detective in his own right, and not Holmes's sidekick. Watson attempts to 'solve' Holmes. What attracted you to making Holmes a focus and a mystery?*
SB: 'Solving' Holmes is key to Watson embracing their partnership and trusting this young man with his life. And as far as I'm concerned, doctors – diagnosticians in particular – are very much detectives, assembling the clues of symptoms to solve the medical mysteries suffered by their patients.

TU: *Holmes restores order by the end of Issue 1, and he effectively prevents the maids and manservants from a series of major thefts. To what extent do you see Holmes as an advocate of order and/or of change?*
SB: Holmes craves order. A mystery is chaos. Perhaps he has a bit of obsessive-compulsive disorder. Discovering and defining clues is all about imposing order upon a chaotic environment like a crime.

TU: *Do you see Holmes as working in aid and/or in opposition to social mobility?*
SB: How's this: in a class-defined society, being the smartest guy in the room is only a feather in one's cap when somebody NEEDS you.

TU: *In 'The "Gloria Scott"' Holmes tells Watson: 'The good fellow [Trevor] was heart-broken at it, and went out to the Terai tea planting, where I hear that he is doing well'. You give a different though equally interesting reading of how Trevor's father's story affected him irrevocably. If Holmes's unveiling of a mystery did not enhance Trevor's well-being, do you feel that we should be more critical of Holmes?*
SB: The 'Gloria Scott' mystery showed Holmes that a life built upon secrets and lies cannot sustain itself. The revelations in that mystery destroyed young Victor Trevor's life as threats from without sought to black-

mail his father. Holmes's first real friend was brought low by the affair, not by Holmes's doing, but as a result of a criminal pact that was destined to be undone. If truth does indeed set free (the maxim *veritas liberat*), then Holmes liberated the elder Trevor from his own guilt and remorse before death claimed him.

TU: *The refrain – '**Once** is happenstance. **Twice** is coincidence. **Thrice** is a pattern of ill intent' – appeared in a number of places and variations, most famously in Ian Fleming's* Goldfinger *(1959). Tell us about this use of anachronism.*
SB: Any retroactive continuity is free to establish that a well-worn phrase might have been uttered much earlier than previously thought. ☺

TU: *What do you see as similarities and differences between Holmes and James Bond?*
SB: I think Bond may have used some of his own fair share of deductive reasoning during his adventures. He certainly had better luck with women than Holmes. Although I'm not sure who would win in a fight …

TU: *Why bring in Irene Adler?*
SB: Well, there was ONE person that Holmes cared about more than mysteries.

TU: *What is next for Holmes?*
SB: That's up to Nick and Joe and Dynamite. We've talked tentatively about an adventure teaming Holmes with a few other dauntless adventurers active during the same era. We'll see …

TU: *Thank you so much for your time, and for writing this excellent series! I look forward to much more* Sherlock Holmes.
SB: And thank YOU for such a lively and thought-provoking examination of our work! ●

Fan Appreciation no.4
Scott Beatty, co-author of Sherlock Holmes: Year One

GO FURTHER

Books

The Young Sherlock Holmes Adventures
Huw-J Davies, Owen Jollands and Jane Straw
(London: Markosia, 2010)

Sherlock Holmes: Year One
Scott Beatty and Daniel Lindro
(Mt. Laurel: Dynamite Entertainment, 2011)

'HE [HOLMES] LOVED
TO LIE IN THE VERY CENTRE OF
FIVE MILLIONS OF PEOPLE,
WITH HIS FILAMENTS
STRETCHING OUT AND
RUNNING THROUGH THEM,
RESPONSIVE TO
EVERY LITTLE RUMOR
OR SUSPICION
OF UNSOLVED CRIME.'

DR. WATSON
'THE RESIDENT PATIENT'

Chapter
6

On Writing New Adventures on Audio: Into the Interstices of Canon

Jonathan Barnes

→ A month or so ago, I made a small yet not wholly insignificant error of judgement. Struggling to teach a class of Creative Writing students the principles of short-story construction and, having exhausted my stock of brisk, accessible, technically adroit tales which might easily be read aloud without the attention of the group wandering too ruinously, I turned, naturally enough, to Arthur Conan Doyle. I turned, in fact, to the briefest entry in the canon, that late account of animal cruelty, violent love and domestic abuse, 'The Adventure of the Veiled Lodger' (1927; Vol. II, pp. 693–704).

Fig. 1: Promotional image for
Big Finish's Sherlock Holmes

While it may not surprise you to learn that the 'Lodger' was not particularly well received, I have always rather admired its air of languid menace, its willingness to hint, quite boldly, at unspeakable acts and its positioning of Holmes not as a mere sleuth but as a kind of moral arbiter, a nineteenth-century Solomon whose injunction against self-murder ('Your life is not your own! Keep your hands off it!') saves Eugenia Ronder from suicide. The group, whose ages spanned from early twenties to retirement, did not generally agree. They found the story to be featureless, thin and fatally lacking in incident. One of them noted, perceptively, that 'Doyle must have been old when he wrote this'. I told her that he had been 70, and she screwed up her face in distaste. 'Wow,' she murmured, 'so he was, like, really old.'

Amongst the prevailing air of incuriosity, however, there was one thing that seemed to seize their imagination and – for it was a warm and rather soupy afternoon – to rouse them for an instant into inspiration. You may recall the passage in question; it appears in the very first paragraph as Watson describes a kind of secret library of Baker Street case files:

There is the long row of year-books which fill a shelf, and there are the dispatch-cases filled with documents, a perfect quarry for the student not only of crime but of the social and official scandals of the late Victorian era. Concerning these latter, I may say that the writers of agonized letters, who beg that the honour of their families or the reputation of famous forebears may not be touched, have nothing to fear. The discretion and high sense of professional honour which have always distinguished my friend are still at work in the choice of these memoirs, and no confidence will be abused. I deprecate, however, in the strongest way the attempts which have been made lately to get at and to destroy these papers. The source of these outrages is known, and if they are repeated I have Mr Holmes' authority for saying that the whole story concerning the politician, the lighthouse and the trained cormorant will be given to the public. There is at least one reader who will understand.

I know, I think, why it was these words which should have inspired that circle of emerging writers because – in its spirit if not in its specifics – it has also inspired me.

In the past year I have been fortunate enough to have been allowed to write a series of Sherlock Holmes pastiches for a company called Big Finish Productions who make

On Writing New Adventures on Audio:
Into the Interstices of Canon
Jonathan Barnes

and distribute full-cast audio dramas, available on CD and through downloads, which are produced to a quality well up to that of Radio 4. The company generates a variety of such prestige dramas, starring not only Holmes but characters from a number of popular works of literature and television, from Dorian Gray to *Doctor Who*, *The Avengers* and *Sapphire and Steel*.

When I joined the firm, they had already produced a range of Sherlock Holmes stories starring Nicholas Briggs as the detective and Richard Earl as Dr Watson. Briggs is one of the most in-demand voice actors in the country, best known for giving life on the small screen to the villainous Daleks and Cybermen of *Doctor Who*, while Earl is a fine, respected theatre actor. Together they form an enjoyably old-fashioned double-act that eschews the subtle revisionism of the Jeremy Brett or Benedict Cumberbatch teams in favour of something altogether more classical. Far more canonical in their approach than Rathbone and Bruce, their performances possess something of the fruity vigour of such earlier radio performers as Carleton Hobbs and Norman Shelley (who played the parts in the long-running BBC radio series of the 1950s) or John Gielgud and Ralph Richardson who took on the roles for producer Harry Alan Towers in an eccentric series of wireless adventures (in one of which Orson Welles, at his most unrestrained, featured as Moriarty). At the time that I became involved, the company had just released a number of extremely faithful adaptations of such canonical texts as *The Hound of the Baskervilles* (1901), 'The Final Problem' and 'The Adventure of the Empty House' as well as some pastiches derived from existing novels and stage plays, including David Stuart Davies's Holmes/Dracula conjunction *The Tangled Skein* and Brian Clemens's full-blooded *Holmes and the Ripper*. The audience is small but loyal and appreciative; the reviews often admiring.

What I was determined to do, however, was to produce pastiches which felt utterly Doylean in their style and approach. In particular, I was keen to set each new story between a pair of canonical adventures in order to provide me with what Holmes might have called 'one fixed point' from which I might extrapolate. The rules that I set myself were as follows: that I should suggest nothing that Doyle himself would not, in my opinion, have attempted (or have been persuaded to attempt) had he the inclination, the time or the perspective. I excluded any characters from other fictions, whether contemporary to Doyle or not. As a result there is to be found no Tarzan of the Apes or Wellsian Martians, no Bunny, Raffles, Carnacki or aged Tiny Tim Cratchit. I also excluded anything that would prove to be genuinely supernatural or physically impossible, taking as my cue Holmes's insistence in 'The Adventure of the Sussex Vampire' that 'this world is big enough for us no ghosts need apply'.

Using as my guide that first-rate chronology to be found in Leslie S. Klinger's three-volume edition of the canon, I found, to my surprise, that it was relatively simple to locate space for my own stories. Curiously, not only was it possible to identify these useful gaps but the exercise itself seemed to require no finessing, no benefit of the doubt, no pushing back the walls of Doyle's invented world. Indeed, the texts themselves seemed almost to encourage such engagement.

My first attempt, *The Adventure of the Perfidious Mariner* (2012), was set at the end of Holmes's documented career in 1912, after 'The Adventure of the Lion's Mane' (Vol. II, pp. 673–93) and before 'His Last Bow: The War Service of Sherlock Holmes'. It takes place in the summer following the disaster of the RMS *Titanic* and features a series of mysterious deaths which centre around a survivor of that tragedy – the real-life manager of the White Star Line, J. Bruce Ismay (played in our production with his customary brilliance by Michael Maloney). Would Doyle ever have placed a real-life event at the heart of a story? Would he have placed a man from the real world at the centre of it? Why not, I concluded? Apart from being a serious writer of historical fiction he was also happy enough to let real-world events form a backdrop to his stories. *A Study in Scarlet* (1887) begins with an accurate precis of what Watson calls 'the second Afghan war' and 'His Last Bow' is set, with propagandistic intent, upon the eve of World War I.

As I began to plot the drama, more and more pieces fell into place. Watson, I decided, should have a personal stake in the sinking; he should have lost someone dear to him on board. A wife, surely? But which one? This is not the place to delve into that particular quagmire except to say that I elected that it should be his second, having found irresistible that implication in 'The Adventure of the Empty House' to do with 'my own sad bereavement'. I also chose to make the piece a study of Holmes and Watson's – at this time somewhat strained – relationship. As Holmes tells us in 'The Adventure of the Lion's Mane,' writing from his lonely villa, 'at this period of my life the good Watson had passed almost beyond my ken.'

Then something struck me, reading again those stories which, in chronological terms, immediately preceded the year 1912 and the single entry which comes afterwards. I am perfectly happy to accept the placing of 'The Adventure of the Creeping Man' as being the last case before Holmes's retirement. In the course of those bizarre events, it seems clear that the doctor and the detective are not perhaps as close as once they were. Consider the terseness of Holmes's telegram ('come at once if convenient – if inconvenient come all the same') and Watson's observations that 'relations between us in those latter days were peculiar' and that 'if I irritated him by a certain methodical slowness in my mentality, that irritation served only to make his own flame-like intuitions and impressions flash up the more vividly and swiftly'. Nonetheless, there is nothing here to suggest that the great man's retirement was imminent.

So, I began to wonder, why does Holmes retire so early? If we are to accept the description in 'His Last Bow' that he is 'a tall, gaunt man of sixty', he can only have been in his early fifties when he retired. There are plenty of theories: Holmes's own, in the first-person narration of 'The Adventure of the Lion's Mane', that he had simply 'given myself up entirely to that soothing life of Nature for which I had so often yearned during the long years spent amid the gloom of London'; the critic Trevor H. Hall's suggestion

On Writing New Adventures on Audio:
Into the Interstices of Canon
Jonathan Barnes

that Holmes was, by this time, suffering 'almost total blindness' as a direct result of 'excessive tobacco use' or the dramatist Bert Coules's implication in his radio adaptation of 'The Adventure of the Retired Colourman' that Holmes had simply fallen out of step with the times, and become rusty, outpaced and outmatched by Barker, 'my hated rival upon the Surrey shore'. I found none of these explanations to be especially satisfying, and so another possibility occurred to me. What if Holmes had made a mistake, some rare error of judgement, far more serious than mine in my choice of reading in that classroom? What if something had gone horribly wrong and he had fled to the Downs in order to escape from it? There is nothing in the canon to disprove such a theory and, if there is nothing concrete to support it either, then we need think only of Watson's discretion, his ability to draw a veil over that which he does not want to reveal. His own love life for example is, as I've already suggested, notoriously obfuscated in his own accounts. Might some failing, even some tragedy, in his old friend not have received similar treatment?

This, then, became the backbone of my story: Holmes in exile from a terrible mistake, a grieving Watson, a man from the real world pursued by demons of his own. Recorded on a bright, clear day last year, in time for the centenary of the *Titanic* sinking, the script was brought to life by a versatile and impressive cast. The reason for Holmes's flight, however, was only hinted at and never revealed in full. With recording finished and the story in the can I knew that it was not yet over between Sherlock Holmes and me. I knew I had to return to Doyle's world and to explore this mystery further.

The result is a more elaborate undertaking – a four-hour box-set of stories called *The Ordeals of Sherlock Holmes* (2013). Each CD contains a single story taken from a different point in Holmes's career. The first, 'The Guttering Candle', set immediately before *A Study in Scarlet*, begins in 1880 with the young Holmes in London (when, as he remarks to Reginald Musgrave in 'The Adventure of the Musgrave Ritual', he has 'taken to living by my wits') and with Watson on duty in Afghanistan. The second story, 'The Adventure of the Gamekeeper's Folly', gives us Holmes and Watson in their pomp, between 'The Adventure of Black Peter' and 'The Adventure of the Bruce-Partington Plans', with Holmes only lately having returned from the Great Hiatus. The third is the story that I've been especially keen to write: a full account of the case which leads to Holmes's retirement, 'The Adventure of the Bermondsey Cutthroats'. The final part of the quartet, 'The Sowers of Despair', takes us beyond even 'His Last Bow', to give us Holmes and Watson after the Great War in 1919, two years before the final run of Holmes stories appeared in *The Strand Magazine*.

The rules were the same as before: to remain as Doylean as possible; to do nothing of which he might not have approved; to tell no type of story that he might not one day, at least in my opinion, have attempted himself. But how are we ever to know such a thing? For are we not told again and again how Doyle had lost interest in his creation, about his fury and his frustration with the detective, his earnest desire for his other

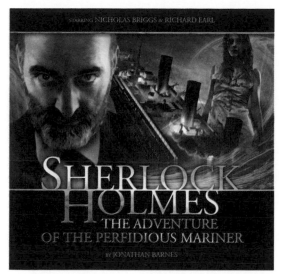

Fig. 2: Cover for Sherlock Holmes: The Adventure of the Perfidious Mariner

works of literature to achieve pre-eminence while Baker Street should be forgotten? He said himself that *The White Company* 'would illuminate our national traditions', while *Sir Nigel* represented 'in my opinion my high-water mark in literature'.

Somehow, however, I have never entirely trusted this version of events. There is too much passion and strangeness in those stories for it to be simply a case of a mature writer being ashamed of some unexpectedly profitable juvenilia. For a man supposedly tired beyond measure of his hero, Doyle was still capable even as late as the 1920s of turning out such deft and surprising fictions as 'The Problem of Thor Bridge' and 'The Adventure of the Illustrious Client'.

Whatever the truth, it seems to me now that Doyle was exceptionally generous-spirited in his creation, even to the extent that he left clues that might lead us to become more than mere readers. Consider, for example, all those cases mentioned but not explained: the disappearance of James Phillimore; Isadora Persano and that remarkable worm; Matilda Briggs and the infamous Great Rat of Sumatra. These are much more, surely, than mere throwaway jokes. Consider, too, those ellipses in the narrative: Watson's personal life, Holmes's background, the secrecy of those long years in Tibet or, as 'Sigerson', hanging out with the head lama or conducting research into coal tar derivatives. Consider those oddities, those peculiar glitches in the texts such as Professor James Moriarty having an identically named brother, the question of Watson's first name or the precise nature of Mycroft's work in the British Government. These moments might be mistaken by the cynical or the unwary as errors made by a too-hasty professional over-eager for the golf course but I would contend that they are not unconscious but *purposeful* opportunities for the writers who were to come after him. They are interstices into which we are actively encouraged to place new adventures. One recalls the telegram of 1896 to William Gillette which contained the notorious injunction to 'marry him or murder or do what you like with him', so often portrayed as a callous wave of the hand from a man with his mind on higher things. In reality, I would contend, that telegram constituted a licence for posterity to extrapolate. It is a pleasing irony, perhaps, that a man who became obsessed with life after death should perpetuate his own for so long through this seeding of his work with opportunities for others to continue his stories once he had passed beyond the veil. Certainly, his presence lingers with those of us today who write new adventures as (and he would surely have relished the comparison) a kind of tutelary spirit.

I think that they were right, then, my students, after their encounter with the enigmatic lodger, to identify that point of interest in the inaugural paragraph. In those pages they discerned the true legacy of Arthur Conan Doyle, his encouraging hints in

On Writing New Adventures on Audio:
Into the Interstices of Canon
Jonathan Barnes

the allusion to the cormorant, the politician and the lighthouse. Across a gulf of almost a century, they heard his exhortation to follow in his footsteps, to write, to contribute, *to imagine*. That choice of story may not have been the error of judgement that I imagined it to be; perhaps, after all, it was the perfect narrative for them to have heard. ●

GO FURTHER

Books

The New Annotated Sherlock Holmes, 3 Volumes
Arthur Conan Doyle
L. S. Klinger (ed.) (New York: W.W. Norton, 2004)

Sherlock Holmes: The Complete Novels and Stories, Volumes I and II
Arthur Conan Doyle
(New York: Bantam, 1986)

Audio plays

The Ordeals of Sherlock Holmes
Jonathan Barnes
(Big Finish, 2013)

The Adventure of the Perfidious Mariner
Jonathan Barnes
(Big Finish, 2012)

'EDUCATION NEVER ENDS, WATSON. IT IS A SERIES OF LESSONS, WITH THE GREATEST FOR THE LAST.'

SHERLOCK HOLMES
'HIS LAST BOW'

Chapter
7

The Creation of 'The Boy Sherlock Holmes'

Shane Peacock

→ It would seem obvious that the first and primary concern of any author starting out on the daunting task of creating the childhood of one of the truly legendary characters in the history of literature would be a deep and abiding interest in that personality. But that was not the case with my creation of The Boy Sherlock Holmes, an award-winning series of novels for young adults (and older, Sherlockian ones as well). The Master, in fact, was nowhere to be seen in the original manuscript for the first novel, *Eye of the Crow* (2007).

Fig. 1: Author Headshot

During speaking engagements, I always tell aspiring writers in search for subjects about which to write that the best method is to pay attention to your own passions. What do you *really* care about? Explore that, and you will find what you want to create and what you *can* write.

Over the years I have written plays, novels, biographies and television documentaries. Themes have emerged in my work. I like larger-than-life characters, historical settings and dramatic events. I am intrigued by human desire, by what motivates individuals, specifically extraordinary ones, who attempt big things and whose lives, writ large, tell us something about ourselves. All my work, from the life story of Farini (who walked over Niagara Falls on a high wire in 1860 and invented the human cannonball act) to my stories for children about an adventurous Canadian boy named Dylan Maples are, in a sense, biographical explorations of remarkable people.

When it came time to create a new work for young readers a few years ago, I was adamant that I would challenge them; create something dark and literary with a deeper subtext. I mined my interests as I searched, considering old ones, finding new ground. I wanted my story to be edgy, a mystery of some sort, set in my favourite time, on the murky streets of Victorian London ('a dense, drizzly fog lay low over the great city,' began Watson's famous description of London at night in *The Sign of the Four* (Vol. I, pp. 121-236); a metropolis that had the most people, the most crime, the greatest ethnic mixture, the most disease, the most celebrities and the most of everything on earth. I knew that Dickens would influence my story and that a gruesome event like a Jack-the-Ripper murder would be at its heart. I also knew that I wanted crows to play a major role. I had studied them while doing research for a magazine article and learned that they were not the flying devils that history, literature and popular imagination proclaimed. Crows and their cousins the ravens, I learned, were the most intelligent of all birds. They are possessed of prodigious brain power, capable of explicitly communicating with each other, of marking the progress of global warming and the West Nile virus and capable of making tools for specific tasks, a talent that no other species besides human beings can demonstrate. I discovered, in short, that I had had a prejudice against crows.

Prejudice was to be the subject at the core of my tale. More than anything else, it drove me to write the story. Prejudice, to me, is the greatest of humanity's sins, the evil behind many of our world's problems. Crows, dark and misunderstood, were a perfect symbol for my novel's central concern. And so I created my narrative. Were I shopping its premise around Hollywood, my pitch would go like this: *A woman is murdered in a dark, foggy alley in the middle of a Victorian London night. No one sees the crime, except for two crows. Based solely on that, a 13-year-old 'half-breed' boy finds the villain.*

The Creation of 'The Boy Sherlock Holmes'
Shane Peacock

My publisher loved the idea, but someone who read the manuscript had a sexy suggestion, one that he wasn't sure would work or that anyone could pull off, but one that had the potential to be sensational. Why not make my character ... Sherlock Holmes? My hero seemed a good deal like him already.

I was reluctant to even consider it at first. It seemed like the commercialization of my serious subject and an invitation to simply use someone else's character. The word 'pastiche' still irritates me but, more importantly, I didn't even like Sherlock Holmes. My memories of him, carried from childhood, were of a stuffy man from a dusty past. But to give it a chance, I read (what I now know as) the 'Canon' from beginning to end ... and was amazed. I couldn't believe what I found: a brilliant character of unfathomable depth, addicted to cocaine, who didn't like women, was a manic depressive, knew the seedy parts of London and, most importantly, who told no one (not even Watson) about his past. 'During my long and intimate acquaintance with Mr. Sherlock Holmes,' says the good doctor as 'The Greek Interpreter' opens, 'I had never heard him refer to his relations, and hardly ever to his own early life.'

It was love at second sight. Here was a larger-than-life character like none other, filled with insecurities that must have had a fascinating genesis. He couldn't have been a to-the-manor-born son of a rich country squire, raised on tea and sweets, unfamiliar with urban squalor and personal tragedies. To me, he was a Londoner, one with serious issues, and obsessed with justice. Who had he *truly* been as a child?

I soon found that Sherlock, with adjustments, was indeed a fit for the disturbed young 13-year-old I had already created, the son of a rich English lady and a poor, brilliant Jewish man that had fallen in love, eloped and lost everything. I went to work on my character and made him, though an unusual take on Holmes, one that could conceivably grow up to be him (though that may not be apparent at first glance). To my delight, the story deepened.

It was my conviction from the start that I would make my tale realistic. I wanted no part in a caricature like the one in the movie *Young Sherlock Holmes* (Barry Levinson, 1985) in which a boyish Watson inexplicably takes part in the story. Casting things in the present tense, I wanted readers to smell the streets of Victorian London, to see its fog, horses and carriages, to be frightened in its East End and sense that this brilliant, ragged boy really lived there. I didn't want my Sherlock to have dreamed of being a detective or anything corny like that. Instead, he becomes involved in a murder investigation by chance and participates, out of necessity, when he is deemed an accomplice. He pursues the solution reluctantly, in great fear, and by my story's end, is compelled by a terrible personal tragedy into a life dedicated to the cause of justice.

The level of research required for such an interpretation was substantial. I reread the canon again, taking notes, reread it once more using Leslie Klinger's *New Annotated Sherlock Holmes* (2006); and studied Dickson Carr's (1949) and Stashower's 1999 Conan Doyle biographies, other Conan Doyle works, Liza Picard's *Victorian London: The*

Fig. 2: Author looking at the Sherlock statue at the Baker Street tube station.

Life of a City, 1840–1870 (2013), and many other histories of the period and accounts of daily life. I revisited the likes of Dickens and Wilkie Collins. I perused books of old photographs, cupping my hands around the images to block out the modern day and attempting to slip right into the Victorian streets. And I went to London, took its wonderful walking tours and sought out not just the old Sherlock sites, but every place that my character went. I investigated the alleys of the East End and timed how long it would take Holmes to walk or run across bridges, to rush from certain parts of the city to others. As I wrote, I began to feel as though I were back in Victorian London, as if I were the boy Sherlock Holmes as he moved, terrified, through the great city in 1867.

I took a great deal of direction from the canon, some from Sherlockian scholarship and a large amount from my imagination for my take on the great man. The Boy Sherlock series is imbued not just with the original character's name but also with the nascent versions of the personality traits and even the physical and sartorial appearance that Conan Doyle gave him. An irregular youth, he wears a suit, though it is threadbare and he is desperate to keep it neat. He is vain, egotistical, brilliant and loves sensational crime stories. He is kind at times. He has an innate ability to deduce the history of others at a glance. He is tall and thin and has grey eyes. His older brother Mycroft has commenced lowly government work and his mother is the daughter of a country squire.

From the Sherlockians I took an 1854 birth date and names like Violet and Sherrinford for members of his family; other touches that only Holmes scholars might appreciate were scattered throughout the texts. But I also made him my own – most notably, he is a part-Jewish 'half-breed', born impoverished into London's lowly Southwark, somewhat ashamed and angry at the world and about who he is. He is the best student in his poor 'national school' but often absent, preferring to roam the streets – his path to university is a tricky one. His dear mother is named Rose ('and so I say again that we have much to hope from the flowers,' says Holmes in 'The Naval Treaty') and his father Wilberforce, after the great British liberator. Were I to pick an adult interpretation of Holmes that best fit my boy, it would have to be Jeremy Brett's from the Granada television series of the 1980s and 1990s. My character, beset by inner demons, could grow up to be his.

There are also ways in which the original version, Sherlockian scholarship and my interpretation blend. As the series opens, Sherlock meets a kindly philanthropist named Andrew C. Doyle (my tip of the hat). Doyle's daughter is named Irene and she and Sherlock, in their youthful way, fall for each other. Their relationship will be tumultuous and one may guess at how it will end. On the streets, Sherlock is wary of a young gang called

The Creation of 'The Boy Sherlock Holmes'
Shane Peacock

Fig. 3: The two Arthur Ellis Award-winning books with their prizes.

The Trafalgar Square Irregulars; at their head is a nasty piece of work named Malefactor ('I have been conscious of some power behind the malefactor,' says Holmes in 'The Final Problem', 'some deep organizing power which forever stands in the way of the law'). He and Sherlock will square off throughout their youth, alike in as many ways as they are different. At Scotland Yard, a detective named Lestrade is another tormentor, much more difficult to deal with than his son, a lad who understands Sherlock to a degree, whose first initial is ... G. But these characters are not just named referentially; they are all on paths to turn into important adults in the life of Sherlock Holmes.

The first novel, *Eye of the Crow*, sets up Sherlock's past and introduces the main players in the series. Its action, which grows more frightening as the story proceeds, ends on a jarring note for a young readers' novel. Thus we come to understand the reason for Sherlock's choice of profession, and the premise for the entire series is stated. Readers see why he will become the man we know so well, why he hates crime and injustice, is wary of relationships with women, and so susceptible to addiction.

The second book in the series, released in 2008 and entitled *Death in the Air*, opens at the Crystal Palace, where Sherlock sees a man fall off a flying trapeze from the glass roof and land, apparently dead, at his feet. The boy notices two cuts in the bar. Soon after, he meets his mentor, an old London apothecary named Sigerson Bell. Though stooped and ancient, this wizard is an expert at deductive diagnosis, martial arts, pugilism, and of course, the effective use of a horsewhip. *Eye of the Crow*'s subtext discussed prejudice and the need for justice; *Death in the Air* addresses the good and evil within us all, as exemplified by the darkness and light within its hero.

The third novel, entitled *Vanishing Girl*, appeared in 2009, and commenced with the kidnapping of Lord Rathbone's daughter. The plot then twists and turns. The text reveals our protagonist's selfishness, his self-centred ways, again so prominent in us all. The six novels in this project (completed by *The Secret Fiend* [2010], *The Dragon Turn* [2011] and the dark, concluding volume *Becoming Holmes* [2012]) bring our irregular hero up to the verge of adulthood. It is my hope that all young readers who experience it will become as fascinated as I now am with Sherlock Holmes. If they benefit from my creation – to even a tiny percentage of Conan Doyle's original work – then I will consider this work an immense success. ●

GO FURTHER

Books

Victorian London: The Life of a City, 1840–1870
Liza Picard
(London: Hachette, 2013)

The New Annotated Sherlock Holmes, 3 Volumes
Arthur Conan Doyle
Leslie S. Klinger (ed.) (New York: W.W. Norton, 2006)

Teller of Tales: The Life of Arthur Conan Doyle
Daniel Stashower
(New York: Henry Holt, 1999)

The Secret Chronicles of Sherlock Holmes
Michael Harrison and June Thompson
(New York: O. Penzler Books, 1994)

Sherlock Holmes: The Complete Novels and Stories, Volumes I and II
Arthur Conan Doyle
(New York: Bantam, 1986)

Book series

The Boy Sherlock Holmes:
Becoming Holmes (2012), *The Dragon's Turn* (2011), *The Secret Fiend* (2010), *Vanishing Girl* (2009), *Death in the Air* (2008), *Eye of the Crow* (2007)
Shane Peacock
(Toronto, ON: Tundra Books)

Fan Appreciation no.5
Robert Ryan, author of *Dead Man's Land*

Interview by Jonathan Cranfield

Robert Ryan's novel *Dead Man's Land* was released in January, 2013. The novel is a murder mystery set largely in the trenches and medical clearing stations of Flanders in 1914. Its hero is an ageing, widowered veteran of the Afghan war, haunted by the memory of a recently-broken friendship, who attempts to unravel the motivations and identity of a killer stalking the members of a front-line Lancashire regiment. Although the novel features characters and references to the Sherlock Holmes stories, it is also a richly-detailed portrait of a world in transition. The political, social, military and industrial upheavals of the early twentieth century all add to the miasma of confusion that attends Dr Watson's investigation of series of gruesome murders.

Jonathan Cranfield: *I have to say that I enjoyed* Dead Man's Land *tremendously and, as a dedicated Holmes fan, it's wonderful to see something more creative and historically-driven being done with the canon rather than the emphasis being solely upon pastiches set in the 'forever 1895' environment. One of the things I most admired was that the novel would appear to have worked equally well if it wasn't set in the Holmesian universe. Did the novel begin life with Watson as the protagonist or was he a subsequent addition?*

Robert Ryan: Ah, that's a perceptive observation and the answer lies very much in the genesis of *Dead Man's Land (DML)*. I had written fourteen books for the publisher Headline, but found that we couldn't agree on the fifteenth. While I was out of contract, I was invited in to see Simon & Schuster. They had an idea for a historical thriller set in the trenches of World War II. I replied that, although it had its merits, the trenches were not a place for a conventional police investigation. Indeed, the Military Police were mainly concerned with desertion and discipline. So I went away and wrote the first 15,000 words of a novel called 'The Bride in Bohemia', which was not intended to have anything to do with the Holmes story 'A Scandal in Bohemia'. It was about a detective with a suffragette wife who is framed for plotting to kill the prime minister (as some suffragettes did), elements of this story remain in *DML*.

Simon & Schuster liked the characters and the plot, but were still insisting on trench warfare. So I said that they didn't want a detective, but a doctor, who might recognize that one of the many fallen soldiers has, in fact been murdered. They liked that. And, furthermore, I said, it should be Dr Watson, of Sherlock Holmes fame. They loved that. I must confess that the germ of that idea had been in my mind for some years, ever since browsing through Jack Tracey's *Encyclopedia Sherlockiana* and

Fan Appreciation no.5
Robert Ryan, author of *Dead Man's Land*

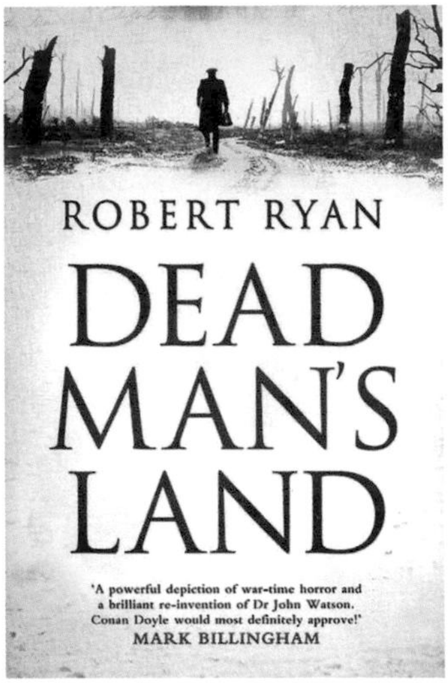

Fig. 1: The cover of Dead Man's
Land blends the conventional
presentation of the contemporary murder mystery with
World War I iconography and
a subtle Holmesian reference
in Dr Watson's medical bag
(Courtesy of Robert Ryan).

coming across a mention that, in 'His Last Bow: The War Service of Sherlock Holmes' (1917), Conan Doyle suggests that Watson would be joining the Royal Army Medical Corps. I did suggest that, although having Watson as the central character would bring added depth and resonance to the novel, it was important that he was in some ways just another medical man. The plot had to work even if he was simply an observant RAMC Major. In the end, Holmes inveigled his way into the story more than initially envisaged, but I would like to think the book could be rewritten without him.

JC: *Holmes initially appears only as a voice in Watson's head, almost taunting him. However, he later becomes integral to the plot and I wondered if you felt tentative about writing in Holmes's 'voice'? Was the idea of a Holmes in decline attractive to you?*

RR: It wasn't so much a worry about writing in Holmes's 'voice' as having him steal the limelight, once more, from his companion. There is a power about Holmes as a character (and icon) that I feared might unbalance or overwhelm the book. On the other hand, I had to address the fact that Watson would feel as if he was missing a limb, particularly as the plot thickened. So the voice is the equivalent of asking 'What would Sherlock do?'

I took no pleasure in the idea of Holmes in decline; it simply seemed a logical progression of the timeline. Although I do admit there is poignancy to the thought of the greatest mind of his generation feeling his faculties are fading. I have always been a huge fan of Peckinpah's westerns, especially *The Wild Bunch* (1969). If you look beyond the violence, they are nearly always concerned with men in the twilight of their life or career. There is a line in the sequel to *DML* that echoes the end of *The Wild Bunch*, when Robert Ryan (the other one) says: 'It won't be like old times but it'll do.' But the main attraction to having Holmes operating somewhat below the peak of his powers is that it gives Watson room to 'breathe' a little more as a character.

JC: *Absolutely, that was particularly striking. I have to ask this next question and you may be as circumspect as you wish! How did you find dealing with the Conan Doyle estate? I have heard many tales on both sides of the current contretemps and I wondered whether that consultation affected the writing process at all?*

RR: To be perfectly frank I have no problem with the rights to Holmes and Watson being 'owned' by an estate or in paying monies for the rights. I just wish it was more clear-cut as regards whom one should pay the money to. During the initial conversations I assumed that, because Conan Doyle died in 1930, the books and characters were out of copyright. I subsequently discovered that they had been trademarked in the European Union by one claimant to the rights and, before writing, I agreed to pay a royalty which I was told would cover me for publication in the United States. It was only much later that I became aware that this was not the case and that a different estate had the US rights because a certain number of the original short stories were in copyright in America (which has a different copyright law thanks, bizarrely, to Sonny Bono). I certainly don't want to go into the legality of all this; it is for the US courts to decide who owns what, which I believe they will in due course. However, ignorance is bliss and during the writing of the book I thought I had an arrangement that gave me the rights to use the characters as I wished, in return for a percentage of any payments and profits. This was extremely fortunate, because, had I realized what a minefield I was blithely strolling through, I might have simply retraced my steps and created another doctor. The US copyright issue only came to the fore after UK publication. However, I think my publishers and that estate have reached an agreement, so I have ploughed on with the sequel to *DML* certain that it can be resolved with all parties kept happy, at least as far as this novel is concerned (which, of course, might be more misplaced optimism).

JC: *So there is going to be a sequel?*

RR: Yes. I always intended to stay with Dr Watson for at least one book after *DML*. However, I knew that I didn't want to repeat the front-line setting. I thought Watson might be traumatized by his experiences. He would suffer if not exactly shell shock, then what we now know at post-traumatic stress including nightmares and mood swings. So, he becomes interested in the treatment of such 'battle nerves' and especially at the contrast between the different methods used to try and cure the officers (rest homes) and men (effectively boot camps to try and 'stiffen their re-

Fan Appreciation no.5
Robert Ryan, author of *Dead Man's Land*

Fig. 2: Still from 'The Blue Carbuncle' (BBC, Season 2, Episode 16, 1968) showing Peter Cushing as Sherlock Holmes and Nigel Stock as Dr Watson

solve'). In the midst of all this he is summoned by a senior politician and asked to investigate the case of a young soldier who has been struck dumb and is virtually catatonic. He shows all the symptoms of shell shock yet has not been near the front. Instead, he was involved in a top secret experiment with seven other men, testing a device 'which could end the war before Christmas'. Watson is then told that an ailing Sherlock Holmes has been interned under the draconian Defence of the Realm Act (DORA). He will only be released if Watson takes on the case.

JC: *From what you've said (and in an entirely non-accusatory way!) I don't think you'd classify yourself as a 'Holmesian'; how do you feel about that term?*

RR: I wouldn't dare claim any such thing. Although nobody who writes crime thrillers with a protagonist of any stripe can escape the long arm of Baker Street and, as with so many writers of my generation, the 'canon' was an important part of my reading life when I was growing up. I don't think I could have done the book unless I retained an abiding affection and admiration for the man and his world. But, oddly, I always felt more Watsonian in persuasion. I think this goes back to the BBC series of the 1960s, when Douglas Wilmer and Peter Cushing both played the Great Detective, but Nigel Stock was a steadfast Watson throughout. I haven't seen it since, but I was at an impressionable age and I recall it as a strong interpretation of the doctor. Perhaps it was helped by the fact that Stock was a genuine ex-military man, having served with the Assam Regiment of the Indian Army and at the bloody Battle of Kohima (his Battle of Maiwand, perhaps). Unlike so many screen Watsons, you believed this man had seen bloody warfare and knew how to use that service revolver. Also, there is something constant, immutable about the character of Holmes throughout the many interpretations whereas Watson is a blank page or a palimpsest to scratch one's own interpretation onto.

JC: *There is a famous piece of criticism about the original Holmes stories that states that one of the reasons for the decline in popularity of the first wave of popular crime fiction was that World War I inured many readers against the shock of murder and loss. Your novel seems to play very consciously with these two different scales of disaster: the personal and the political. I wondered if this was a self-conscious decision to set a murder mystery somewhere where the value of life was so cheap?*
RR: Yes it was, it had several strong elements as regards a crime setting. What better place to get away with murder than a battlefield, especially one where up to 20,000 men could die in a single day? Why bother with the effort of tracking down a murderer, especially when the chances of them surviving the war were so slim? If the culprit was an officer, the average life span at the front was six weeks. Why not just let the everyday attrition take its toll? But, of course, the doctor is not the sort of man to let such considerations cloud his judgement in seeking justice.

However, I then realized that all of this equally applied to the murderer. Why bother killing men who probably only had days or weeks left anyway? Surely it would be easier just to see who survived the war and pick them off? Which is why I had to give the murderer a motive not just for the killings, but for wanting the men to know why they are being singled out to die in the midst of mass slaughter. So, as a setting, it really did make me wonder about the value that could be placed on a single human life and also the urge for revenge that transcends the cold hard facts.

JC: *The descriptions of medical care during the war are very striking. As a reader, it seemed to me that the lives of the nurses were a key component*

Fan Appreciation no.5
Robert Ryan, author of *Dead Man's Land*

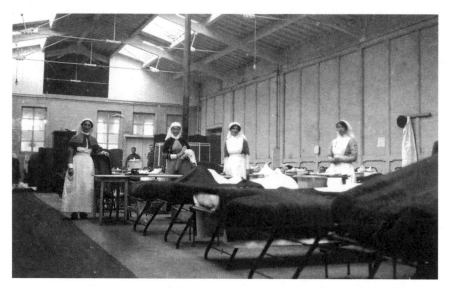

Fig. 3: No. 13 Stationary Hospital in Boulogne (Courtesy of Ruby Cockburn, British Red Cross Society).

of this story for you. Was this the case and did it require much historical research to make the depiction legitimate? Is this a forgotten story, if you like, from the period?

RR: When I set about researching the novel, I knew I had three elements I had to get right or I'd get letters. One was the war in the trenches, which has been documented in minute detail and was in fact relatively straightforward (with a little help from the Imperial War Museum). Another was placing the story correctly within the Holmes canon, in terms of chronology and characters at least. I knew I had little leeway there apart from a helping hand thanks to Conan Doyle's vagueness with things such as Watson's marriages. Finally, I had to get the medical situation at the front-line correct. Like many people, most of my knowledge of World War I medical treatment came from *Testament of Youth* by Vera Brittain. She was a VAD, a member of the Voluntary Aid Detachment, women, mostly, but not exclusively, from well-to-do backgrounds, who volunteered as auxiliaries. They made tea, washed dressings, scrubbed floors, fed the patients and tended to be looked down upon by trained nurses from Queen Alexandra's Imperial Military Nursing Service, aka QAs. It is not exactly a forgotten story, but the hierarchy and various rivalries (VADs vs QAs vs Canadian, American and Australian nurses) has been rather obscured over the years, especially with the emphasis on front-line

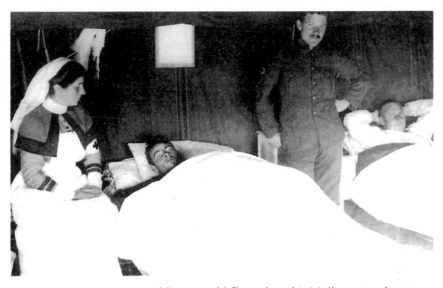

Fig. 3: A Casualty Clearing
Station in Flanders, 1915
(Courtesy of Ruby Cockburn,
British Red Cross Society).

soldiers, and I floundered initially as to what type of nurse would be where.

My breakthrough came when I found *This Intrepid Band*, a wonderful online source of information about the medical services in World War I. Its archive includes a great many letters from serving nurses during World War I, an important resource for the novel. I met Sue Light who runs the blog and she gave me pointers on how the medical service worked, where you would find nurses (not at the frontline, but in Casualty Clearing Stations, some way behind the lines), the types of wounds they would have to deal with, as well as their (limited, if you were a British nurse) social life. She also fed me pages from issues of the *British Medical Journal* published during the war, which helped formulate the idea that Watson could be in the RAMC, despite his advanced age, because he had become an expert in the new-fangled methods of blood transfusion. I do suspect there is a novel or TV series (*Call the VAD?*) to be written concentrating solely on these remarkable women and their stories. I hardly scraped the surface.

JC: *Your novel shows a world turned upside down in terms of class and sexual politics as well as through the war itself. The depiction of unionized labour and the suffragette movement seem particularly designed to*

Fan Appreciation no.5
Robert Ryan, author of *Dead Man's Land*

draw attention to the Holmesian world as fading anachronism. Watson describes himself as feeling 'Victorian' at one point. Was this part of your thinking?

RR: There is something affecting and fascinating about the end of eras and empires. We all know that World War I swept away a 'Golden Generation' of young men, but it had other profound effects: women in the workplace (and at war), the upper classes engaging with the lower in the trenches, and geographical boundaries being breached with men from different parts of the country (and with mutually incomprehensible dialects) were often thrown together. So by 1918 the world was very different from that of 1895, far more removed than we are from, say, 1990. I think I wanted to emphasize that Watson, a thoroughly decent man, knows that his values are from another age. He will struggle with concepts such as emancipation, divorce and sexual freedoms. Watson's challenge is to try and see this new world through younger eyes, but he is only too well aware that he is, like his old friend and companion, a man out of time. ●

Acknowledgements
Like Robert himself, the interviewer would like to thank Sue Light (the author of the This Intrepid Band blog) for her kind cooperation and help with identifying relevant images and allowing their reproduction.

GO FURTHER

Books

Dead Man's Land
Robert Ryan
(London: Simon & Schuster, 2013)

Testament of Youth
Vera Brittain
(Harmondsworth: Penguin Classics, 2005)

Online

This Intrepid Band [Blogspot], http://greatwarnurses.blogspot.co.uk/

Chapter
8

Getting Level with the King-Devil: Moriarty, Modernity and Conspiracy

Benjamin Poore

→ 'Do you tell me that we have to sit down under this? Do you say that no-one can ever get level with this king-devil?'
'No, I don't say that,' said Holmes, and his eyes seemed to be looking far into the future. 'I don't say that he can't be beat. But you must give me time – you must give me time!'
(Epilogue to *The Valley of Fear*, 1914)

Introduction

In the *Elementary* episode 'The Red Team' (Robert Doherty, CBS, 2012 -, Series 1, Episode 13), Jonny Lee Miller's New York-based Sherlock is revealed to have covered one wall of the brownstone that he shares with Joan Watson in clues and information relating to Moriarty; Watson refers to this as his 'wall of crazy'. Yet despite Holmes's obsessive search for the master-criminal in whom few believe, the detective is dismissive of conspiracy theories. Indeed, Sherlock says his hobby is 'conspiracy theor*ists*. I adore them, as one would a barmy uncle, or a pet that can't stop walking into walls'. The writers of this episode (Jeffrey Paul King and Craig Sweeny) are surely aware of the dual irony here. Not only will Moriarty turn out to be 'real', but also the 'red team' conspiracy investigated by Holmes's online conspiracy-theorist acquaintance, 'Zapruder', happens to be true. So Holmes rejects the existence of conspiracy theories in general, while accepting certain conspiracies in the particular.

The show's knowing, double-edged treatment of covert activities and secret organizations is indicative of the game that *Elementary* continues to play with Sherlockian fan knowledge. The first episodes of *Elementary* aired after both the first two Guy Ritchie Sherlock Holmes films and Series 1 and 2 of the BBC's *Sherlock* (Mark Gatiss and Steven Moffat, 2010-). Fans of the canon and its adaptations are therefore primed to spot the cross-references and differences between the series, especially following the well-publicized objections of *Sherlock*'s producer, Sue Vertue, to *Elementary*, as noted by Porter.[1] On a deeper level, the writers and the show's creator, Robert Doherty, must also be aware that conspiracy pervades the canon's central incident, the presumed death of Sherlock Holmes at the hands of his archenemy, Professor Moriarty.

In this chapter, I want to explore some of the ways in which conspiracy thinking is both general to the canon, and particular to the issue of Moriarty. From there, I will touch on the idea of fans and readers of the canon as co-conspirators and then consider how the Guy Ritchie films and the BBC *Sherlock* place Moriarty at the centre of different types of conspiracy. The chapter will argue that Moriarty's position as the recurring chief of a vast conspiracy was a way for the Holmes canon and its readers to apprehend the frightening uncertainties of modernity. Twenty-first century Holmes fandom, by contrast, moves with ease between the fictional and the factual, and between different adaptations, giving different accounts of the same central events, and understanding the Moriarty conspiracy to be both true and false.

The misfiring canon

What I want to argue, to begin with, is that the invention of Moriarty by Conan Doyle in 1893, as a narrative tool with which to kill off Holmes, was a move which backfired spectacularly. Close reading of 'The Final Problem' (1893; Vol. 1, pp.713-748) raises many problems that make the story – that is, Watson's statement of the case – anything but final. To give a brief overview of some of the key issues: how can we trust Watson's ac-

Getting Level with the King-Devil:
Moriarty, Modernity and Conspiracy
Benjamin Poore

Fig. 1: Badges of belonging: Sherlock merchandise indicating familiarity with the 'Moriarty Was Real' and 'I believe' memes (from author's own collection).

count when he wasn't present at the crucial struggle? Can we trust the note supposedly left by Holmes at the precipice? Does Holmes's own description of Moriarty as the Napoleon of Crime, 'the organizer of half that is evil and nearly all that is undetected in this great city', ring true, especially when it is introduced so late in the canon? Have all the adventures up to this point, by extraordinary luck, not concerned Moriarty? Or has Holmes been keeping the reality of the situation from Watson, or Watson keeping it from the reader?

With hindsight, we can say that in his attempts to kill off Holmes using a shadowy criminal figure, Conan Doyle only succeeded in generating hundreds of theories, pastiches and other fictional attempts to fill in the blanks of the story. As post-structuralism recognized, language will never quite do our bidding, never simply say what we want it to say. In that sense, 'The Final Problem' could be said to beautifully evoke Barthes's notion of the ideal text, both readerly and writerly, a fulfilment of the goal to make the reader:

> no longer a consumer but a producer of the text [...] this text is a galaxy of signifiers, not a structure of signifieds; it has no beginning; it is reversible; we gain access to it by several entrances, none of which can be authoritatively declared to be the main one.

It could be said, therefore, that Conan Doyle's attempt on Holmes's life, intended as an act of destruction, has instead fuelled more than a century of creativity, of speculative rewritings of 'The Final Problem'.

A criminal conspiracy

In a previous essay, I classified Holmes pastiches as either 'faith-breakers' or 'faith-healers': either adaptations that threaten the basic principles of the Holmes universe as we know it, or else adaptations which attempt to bring harmony and cohesion to the world of Holmes by establishing a new setting and/or a new set of rules. I argued that believing in Sherlock Holmes – in his supposed deductive powers – was as much an act of faith as one of logic; we need to believe that such a man can make sense of, and keep order in, a chaotic world. But a belief in a scientific messiah for the modern age also implies a belief in a modern Satan, a correspondingly evil force that, like Sherlock's deductive powers, cannot be fully explained by the observable facts. To return to that famous statement of Holmes's, quoted above: he claims that Moriarty 'is the organizer of half that is evil and nearly all that is undetected in this great city'. Does that mean 'undetected' by Holmes, too? Is Holmes arguing that nearly all the crimes that he has no knowledge of are committed by Moriarty and his men? Surely Holmes is here committing the fallacy of *petitio principii* (begging the question). He is following classic inductive conspiracy-theory logic that the lack of evidence for a hypothesis, assumed a priori to be correct, is due to a ruthlessly efficient cover-up, rather than the hypothesis being wrong. Certainly, Holmes's reported conversation with Moriarty in 'The Final Problem' would appear to back up the idea of the detective interfering with a complex criminal conspiracy: the Professor claims that his operations have been successively 'incommoded', 'inconvenienced' and 'absolutely hampered'. From Moriarty's perspective, Holmes's incursions may seem, conversely, like a conspiracy against him. Moriarty may, however, be bluffing, pretending that Holmes has been more successful than he has in order to throw him off the trail. And besides, Holmes's power is not meant to reside in his ability to extract vague confessions from wrongdoers, but to prove what they did and how.[2]

Therefore, it seems that the logical end of journeying through the canon aboard the ship of Sherlockian reasoning is to have one's deductive apparatus smashed to pieces on the rocks of Moriarty, a ghostly presence who ought not to exist but does; whose presence must be induced and invented, rather than deduced. If most Holmes stories appeared to offer the late-Victorian reader the comforting idea that the modern world can, after all, be 'read' and understood through properly observing, rather than seeing, as noted by Jaffe and Jann, then the Moriarty Problem is that in 1893, at the height of his powers, Holmes confronts a power network that he cannot capture or destroy: cannot apprehend, in either sense of the word. And, though he thinks he has destroyed the chief intellect behind this conspiracy (and, in 'The Adventure of the Empty House' (1903; Vol. 2, pp.781-828), neutralized his deputy, Colonel Moran), if the criminal conspiracy still exists, then Holmes only continues to operate, after the hiatus, 'on licence', by some arrangement that he will not probe too deeply. As he rather enigmatically – or evasively – says of Moriarty and the eighteenth-century criminal Jonathan Wild, 'Everything comes in circles [...] The old wheel turns and the same spoke comes up. It's all been done before, and will be again.' His comment might be taken as a hint that Jonathan Wild and Moriarty stand as representatives of the 'hidden force' that has always dominated London crime.

The conspiracy mindset and modernity

It is significant that Moriarty comes to challenge Holmes's benevolent surveillance and knowledge of the city at the very end of the nineteenth century, when, as noted by Beckson, cultural narratives of decline, and fears of insurrection, anarchism, degeneration and atavism, were attached to the sprawling metropolis of London, with its extremes of wealth and abject poverty. It is not too much of a stretch, I would suggest, to see the modern metropolis as the breeding-ground for modern feelings of paranoia, anxiety, isolation, morbidity, impotence, existential insignificance, and of being adrift in a society overloaded with information in which it feels impossible to really know anything. These symptoms of modernity would certainly have been recognized by founders

Getting Level with the King-Devil:
Moriarty, Modernity and Conspiracy
Benjamin Poore

of social science such as Max Weber and Émile Durkheim. It is also a pattern, of course, that we can find in most of the writers of the early twentieth century classed as modernists. However, the sense of being cut adrift from intellectual and spiritual certainties, and alienated by the vast, unknowable modern city, are certainly also discernible in Victorian thought and writing; long before Eliot's *The Waste Land* (1922), there was, for example, Matthew Arnold's *Dover Beach* (1867) lamenting the 'melancholy, long, withdrawing roar' of the 'sea of faith').[3]

There is also an important sense, however, in which the conspiracy theories that we recognize, and often deride, from the last hundred years – the assassinations of JFK, RFK and MLK, the 'faked' moon landings, Princess Diana's death as a royal 'hit', 9/11 'truther' theories, Obama 'birther' theories – are also reactions to the condition of modernity. Newheiser, Farias and Tausch, surveying the research, note that 'social anomie, lack of trust, and feelings of powerlessness are amongst the predictors of conspiracy beliefs' while later referring to 'the need to protect oneself from the anxiety and meaninglessness resulting from awareness of mortality'. Aupers adds to this picture that the development of increasingly opaque and autonomous social systems, and ever-expanding bureaucracies, fuel conspiracist paranoia and suggests that conspiracy theorizing can be seen as 'a hybrid of scepticism and belief – as a "religion for atheists" or a form of rational enchantment'. Furthermore, Aupers insists, it is 'epistemological insecurity' that is both the 'cause and consequence of a proliferating conspiracy culture', and notes that these trends have been discussed by social scientists since the nineteenth century. David Aaronovitch, in his popular study of conspiracy theories, *Voodoo Histories* (2009), ends by suggesting that conspiracists' paranoia may be 'the sticking plaster that we affix to an altogether more painful wound', that of 'feeling ourselves to be of no importance whatsoever, and our lives (and especially our deaths) of little real significance except to ourselves'.

Moriarty's status as would-be conspirator behind an early start to World War II, as shown in *A Game of Shadows* (Guy Ritchie, 2011), is particularly interesting in the light of the above, because of the theory that the Great War was engineered by a shadowy cabal of Jewish business interests who stood to profit from it, which began to be widely circulated as 'The Protocols of the Elders of Zion' in Germany in 1919, noted by Aaronivitch. The book was influential on Nazi ideas of the so-called 'stab in the back' that had supposedly prevented a German victory in 1918, and which was used to justify re-armament and the victimization of the Jews. By substituting Professor Moriarty for the Jews, *A Game of Shadows* removes the scurrilous anti-Semitism but leaves the conspiracy itself intact.

Nevertheless, perhaps what differentiates *A Game of Shadows*'s Moriarty and *Sherlock*'s Jim Moriarty so strongly from the canonical Professor is that, to borrow the phraseology of the Joker in *The Dark Knight* (Christopher Nolan, 2008), they are 'agent[s] of chaos', criminals who want to introduce anarchy and instability to the system, either

———

Fig. 2: Sherlock Holmes bat-
tlos with Professor Moriarty
at the Reichenbach Falls,
in Sidney Paget's illustration for 'The Final Problem',
published in The Strand
Magazine, December 1893.

for personal profit, or to gain Sherlock's attention. This change suggests – if the screenwriters have judged their public correctly – that what we most fear today is not so much the shadowy organization, secretly exercising control. After all, exposure to so many conspiracy theories, amplified by the Internet, means they no longer have the power to shock us (and anyway, one person's conspiracy theory is another person's ideologically-motivated view of how the world works: is the world banking system a global conspiracy? Is the IMF?). Instead, the primary fear with which we associate these contemporary Moriartys is their ability to upset the world order rather than rig it; to inflict random violence and panic on the civilian, the innocent.

Conspiracy theories in film

However, one problem with conspiracies and villains in movie franchises is that, once the villain is revealed, there is a tendency to try to go one higher in the sequel(s), to show that the criminal boss is only the deputy of the 'big boss': thus, Star Wars (George Lucas, 1977) has the seemingly all-powerful Darth Vader, until he is revealed to defer to the Emperor Palpatine in the film's sequels. While the first Twilight film (Catherine Hardwicke, 2008) features three 'bad' vampires, James, Victoria and Laurent, the film's sequels focus on the supposedly super-powerful (but largely ineffective) Volturi. The latest Batman trilogy (Christopher Nolan, 2008–12) has a secret society, the League of Shadows, which, for thousands of years, has destroyed civilizations all over the world when they are judged to be irredeemably corrupt. In a way, this is the logic of the video game bleeding into films which are often prime candidates themselves for video-game licensing deals. The structure of most video games is that a 'level boss' must be defeated to complete that level and move onto the next, and the bosses become tougher to beat, requiring more skill, speed, firepower and energy to defeat in the game's final stages, culminating in the 'game boss', who often uses the powers of several of the previous level bosses combined.

Moriarty has not been immune to this super-sizing process; his on-screen activities over the past few years at least begin to justify the rather hyperbolic assertion of Barker (quoted in this chapter's title and epigraph) that Moriarty is a 'king-devil'. Moriarty's scheme in A Game of Shadows is truly international, with the Reichenbach Falls being not a remote wilderness but the site of an international summit. In Sherlock, Jim Moriarty engages an international squad of hit men with which to threaten the lives of Holmes and his friends. The reason I raise this as a problem is that hero and villain can

Getting Level with the King-Devil:
Moriarty, Modernity and Conspiracy
Benjamin Poore

Fig. 3: Jim Moriarty in Sherlock uses his knowledge of how a sprawling, chaotic London works, in order to commit blatant crimes in 'The Reichenbach Fall'.

no longer be each other's direct counterpart if the villain is merely a 'level boss'; Holmes and Moriarty only fit together if both are locked in a struggle for supremacy over London or England. Jim Moriarty, in particular, is potentially diminished by his association with other criminal gangs, becoming a small fish in a big pond. The third series of Sherlock has responded radically to the challenge of where to go after its climactic series 2 encounter with Moriarty – in a manner which has divided viewers and critics. Nevertheless, series 3's deeper exploration of the central characters did not mean that it relinquished its preoccupation with criminal conspiracies and evil masterminds. The same is likely to be true of the mooted third film in the Guy Ritchie series, if it does appear.

Moriarty was real

There is a further twist, however, to the reinvention of Moriarty as agent of chaos, rather than elusive head of a criminal enterprise. Jim Moriarty uses his knowledge of how a sprawling, chaotic London works not only to commit blatant crimes and then walk free from his trial in 'The Reichenbach Fall' (*Sherlock* Series 2 Episode 3), but also to frame Sherlock as a fantasist who pays actors to play along with the idea that he is a brilliant detective. His neat inversion of the truth, and people's gullibility in accepting it, can be read as an implicit comment on the public's willingness to swallow superficially plausible conspiracy theories.[5] It is notable that, particularly in the second series finale, and in contrast to the expansive ambitions of Moriarty in *A Game of Shadows*, Jim Moriarty's motives are personal rather than on a larger, conspiratorial scale.

Moriarty's actions also spawned a hugely successful fan 'meme', the phrase 'Moriarty Was Real', which often appears on fanart and merchandise alongside the statement 'I believe in Sherlock Holmes'. The latter assertion has even been known to find its way into street graffiti and the Conan Doyle sections of bookshops. These appearances of 'Moriarty Was Real' and 'I believe' in the urban landscape are documented in numerous Twitter accounts and on Facebook 'group', 'movement' and even 'cause' pages, named using variations of these phrases. As such, 'Moriarty Was Real' functions as a (sometimes literal) badge of belonging to be exchanged between fans: a counter-conspiracy, since it pits fan knowledge and faith (in the character, in his ability to cheat death, in a third series) against Moriarty's invented conspiracy which matches his real circulation of a conspiracy theory about Sherlock. This is an elegant illustration of Barthes's notion of the ideal text, mentioned above: 'it has no beginning; it is reversible; we gain access to it by several entrances, none of which can be authoritatively declared to be the main one.' *Sherlock* reverses the original order of Moriarty as criminal and deceiver, and Holmes as

Fig. 4: Jim Moriarty in Sherlock goes to great lengths—and seemingly has the city at his beck and call—to place the message 'I.O.U.' on display where Sherlock might see it.

Fig. 5: 'I.O.U' graffiti on Baker Street in 'The Reichenbach Fall'. The 'I.O.U.' messages in the episode are echoed by fans' real-life placement of 'I believe in Sherlock Holmes' and 'Moriarty Was Real' in the urban landscape.

Fig. 6: Holmes and Moriarty meet and play chess at the international summit at Reichenbach in A Game of Shadows.

hero, while the fans reverse it back.[6] Passing on the 'meme' of 'I believe in Sherlock Holmes' is also a neat inversion of the phenomenon of the young men who reportedly wore black armbands in mourning for Holmes after 'The Final Problem' was published, as noted by Lycett.

Inevitably, references to the fan counter-conspiracy also find their way back into *Elementary*: in 'A Loaded Gun, Filled with Drugs' (Series 1, Episode 15), Sherlock's old dealer friend, Rhys, declares significantly, twice, 'I believe in Sherlock Holmes'; in the very next scene, Joan Watson is shown peeling a red apple, of the sort into which Jim Moriarty in *Sherlock* carves the letters 'I.O.U', and Sherlock eats a piece of peel. This is, perhaps, an apt visual metaphor for the way that *Sherlock* fans watching *Elementary* are consuming *Sherlock* shavings.

Despite Sue Vertue's professional concern regarding the similarities between the two shows, after the headline-grabbing casting of Jonny Lee Miller and cameo appearances by British actors John Hannah (Series 1, Episode 15) and Vinnie Jones (Series 1, Episode 12), the two series have diverged considerably, playing up different elements of the canonical and extra-canonical Holmes.[7] For instance, where Benedict Cumberbatch's Sherlock in *Sherlock* identifies himself as a 'high-functioning sociopath' ('A Study in Pink', Series 1 Episode 1), and Watson is credited with bringing out his warm, more 'human' side, as Scott-Zechlin has noted, Miller's Sherlock is a recovering drug addict (playing up the canon's references to Holmes's cocaine use) and Watson is initially employed by his father as Sherlock's 'sober companion' (Series 1, Episode 1). And while John often has to counter the assertion that he and Sherlock are lovers in *Sherlock*, as Lavigne points out, Jonny Lee Miller's Sherlock is simultaneously (re-)heterosexualized, and also, to an extent, *de*sexualized, by his apparent lack of sexual interest in his co-habitee, Joan Watson (Lucy Liu). Additionally, the figure of Irene Adler, while repeatedly invoked in both, seems to have an unconventional ongoing association with Moriarty in *Sherlock* ('A Scandal in Belgravia', Series 2, Episode 1), while in *Elementary* – although Moriarty is supposed to have killed her – the first series leads up to the climactic revelation that Adler is alive, and moreover, she actually *is* Moriarty.[8] Perhaps most noticeably for the regular viewer, *Elementary* follows the successful US 'police procedural' model, often opening with a murder and a crime scene, whereas *Sherlock* has longer episodes, with much less emphasis on serial murder cases, and which lead, in all three series so far, to a third-episode confrontation with the master-criminal. Much more could be written about how *Sherlock*, given its production context, has a good deal in common with the revamped *Doctor Who* (Sydney Newman, BBC TV, 1963 -) (in which *Sherlock* creators Mark Gatiss and Steven Moffat are also key players). By contrast, *Elementary* owes far more to US crime dramas such as *Dexter* (James Manos, Jnr et al, Showtime, 2006-13),

Getting Level with the King-Devil:
Moriarty, Modernity and Conspiracy
Benjamin Poore

Castle (Andrew W. Marlowe, ABC, 2009–) and *The Mentalist* (Bruno Heller, CBS, 2008–) than to its British counterpart.

The comparative exercise carried out in the previous paragraph emphasizes the plurality of Holmes adaptations: there cannot have been a time since the characters' invention that three different, very high-profile adaptations have been simultaneously developing across TV and film. Instead of seeing one master-plot, audiences are able to compare how different elements of the Holmes mythos are seeded, de-emphasized or updated. After all (and despite the prevalence of 9/11, Osama and Obama conspiracy theories online), grand, totalizing master narratives are very twentieth century, as Lyotard long ago proclaimed. Audiences, fans in particular, are not locked into one fictional world but able to freewheel between them, playing the game of conspiracies and hidden significances (did the appearance of Joan's apple matter?), replaying and discussing details and incidents with others. They are also well aware of the industry dynamics behind the casting, shooting and running of these shows. This multiplicity of standpoints from which to view Holmes and Moriarty's activities suits the porous boundary-crossing tenor of the times, where the Internet has increased the ways in which we commingle reality and fiction, and commingle 'official' canonical fiction with fanfiction. And after all, in the 2010s, as the protracted effects of the global banking crisis play out, perhaps the more prevalent fear is not that some mastermind has secret plans for all of us, but that no one has a plan: that democracy and capitalism's crises of legitimacy will themselves generate the anarchy that these modern Moriartys crave. ●

Notes

1. Lynette Porter quotes Vertue as saying, 'We have been in touch with CBS and informed them that we will be looking at their finished pilot very closely for any infringement of our rights.'
2. Then again, there are no independent witnesses to this account and only Holmes's word that it took place, a key point in the 'Moriarty is imaginary' school of interpreting 'The Final Problem'.
3. Joseph McLaughlin's *Writing the Urban Jungle* (2000) also makes a case for Conan Doyle's affinities with modernism, suggesting that Doyle reconfigures London as 'a frontier space' under threat of invasions from abroad, arguing for the experimental quality of *A Study in Scarlet* (1887) for its '*juxtaposition* of two stories and two locations', and revealing their interdependence.
4. See the 'Final Boss' entry on the *TV Tropes* wiki for a range of final boss permutations.
5. As noted by Hodgson, Moriarty's ploy could even be read as a comment on fans of the canon who are invited to venerate (in more or less serious ways) a reasoning model that turns out, on occasion, to be nonsensical.
6. To further develop a reading of Barthes's statement, fans gain access to the Sherlock Holmes universe(s) by 'several entrances', through the texts mentioned above,

or perhaps as children through the animated Holmes/science fiction mash-up, *Sherlock Holmes in the 22nd Century* (Sandy Ross, STV, 1999–2001), through the canon, or through *Sherlock, Elementary*, or the films. Furthermore, despite the account of Holmes and Watson's meeting given in *A Study in Scarlet*, the graphic novel *Sherlock Holmes: Year One* (Scott Beatty and Daniel Indro, 2011) posits a different order of events, and of course Andrew Lane's Young Sherlock Holmes series presents a whole series of pre-canonical adventures for the detective, as does Shane Peacock's The Boy Sherlock Holmes series and Castalia, Davies, Straw and Jolland's 2009 *The Young Sherlock Holmes Adventures* comic book. This interest in positing as-yet-untold versions of Holmes's childhood is explained by Shane Peacock, in conversation with Tom Ue, in terms of a conspiracy of silence: if Holmes never tells anyone about his past, then he must be 'for some unknown reason, hiding it'. The need to fill in these silences and gaps is, of course, closely linked to the contemporary, popular Freudian belief that childhood experiences and traumas explain adult behaviour. Hence, Peacock characterizes the adult Sherlock as 'messed up', leading inevitably to the question, 'What sort of childhood did he have?'

7. The casting of Miller was headline-grabbing, of course, because Miller had played alongside Cumberbatch in the 2011 National Theatre production of *Frankenstein* in London, with both actors playing Victor Frankenstein and the monster on alternate nights.

8. The Guy Ritchie films *Sherlock Holmes* (2009) and *A Game of Shadows* take a position mid-way between the two TV series regarding their development of Irene Adler: who and Sherlock were in an ongoing relationship, and Moriarty killed her.

~~~~~~~~~~

GO FURTHER

Books

Sherlock Holmes: Year One
Scott Beatty and Daniel Indro
(Runnemede, NJ: Dynamite Entertainment, 2011)

Eye of the Crow (The Boy Sherlock Holmes series #1)
Shane Peacock
(Toronto: Tundra Books, 2011)

Voodoo Histories: How conspiracy theory has shaped modern history
David Aaronovitch
(London: Vintage Books, 2010)

Getting Level with the King-Devil:
Moriarty, Modernity and Conspiracy
Benjamin Poore

Death Cloud (Young Sherlock Holmes series #1)
Andrew Lane
(Basingstoke: Macmillan, 2010)

The Young Sherlock Holmes Adventures
Drew Castalia, Huw-J. Davies, J. L. Straw and Owen Jollands
(London: Markosia, 2010)

The Man Who Created Sherlock Holmes: The Life and Times of Sir Arthur Conan Doyle
Andrew Lycett
(New York: Free Press, 2007)

The New Annotated Sherlock Holmes, 3 Volumes
Arthur Conan Doyle
Leslie S. Klinger (ed.) (New York: W.W. Norton, 2004)

Writing the Urban Jungle: Reading Empire in London from Doyle to Eliot
Joseph McLaughlin
(Charlottesville, VA: University of Virginia Press, 2000)

The Waste Land, Prufrock and other Poems
Thomas Stearns Eliot
(Mineola, NY: Dover, 1998)

London in the 1890s: A cultural history
Karl Beckson
(New York, W.W. Norton, 1992)

S/Z
Roland Barthes
(New York: Hill and Wang, 1974)

Extracts/Essays/Articles
'"Trust no one": Modernization, paranoia and conspiracy culture'
Stef Aupers
In *European Journal of Communication*. 27: 22 (2012), pp. 22–34.

'Sherlock Holmes and the Leap of Faith: The Forces of Fandom and Convergence in Adaptations of the Holmes and Watson Stories'

Benjamin Poore
In *Adaptation* 6:2 (2013), pp. 158-171[first published online, 24 September 2012]

'The Noble Bachelor and the Crooked Man'
Carlen Lavigne
In Lynette Porter (ed.). *Sherlock Holmes for the 21st century: Essays on new Adaptations* (Jefferson, NC: McFarland, 2012), pp. 13-23.

'The Process of Elimination: The Americanization of Sherlock Holmes'
Lynette Porter
In Lynette Porter (ed.). *Sherlock Holmes for the 21st century: Essays on new Adaptations* (Jefferson, NC: McFarland, 2012) pp.113-27.

'"But It's the Solar System!" Reconciling Science and Faith through Astronomy'
Ariana Scott-Zechlin
In Louisa Ellen E. Stein and Kristina Busse (eds). *Sherlock and Transmedia Fandom* (Jefferson, NC: McFarland, 2012), pp. 56-69.

'The functional nature of conspiracy beliefs: Examining the underpinnings of belief in the Da Vinci Code conspiracy'
Anna Newheiser, Miguel Farias and Nicole Tausch
In *Personality and Individual Differences*. 51: 8 (2011), pp. 1007-11.

'The Boy Wonder: A Conversation with Shane Peacock'
Tom Ue
In *The Baker Street Journal*. 60:3 (2010), pp. 33-40

'Dover Beach'
Matthew Arnold
In Nicholas Shrimpton (ed). *Matthew Arnold: Everyman's Poetry* (London: J.M. Dent, 1998), p. 78.

'The Recoil of "The Speckled Band": Detective Story and Detective Discourse'
John A. Hodgson
In *Poetics Today*. 13: 2 (1992), pp. 309-24.

'Detecting the Beggar: Arthur Conan Doyle, Henry Mayhew, and "The Man with the Twisted Lip"'
Audrey Jaffe
In *Representations*. 31: 2 (1990), pp. 96-117.

Getting Level with the King-Devil:
Moriarty, Modernity and Conspiracy
Benjamin Poore

'Sherlock Holmes Codes the Social Body'
Rosemary Jann
In *ELH*. 57: 3 (1990), pp. 685–708.

Film/Television

'The Red Team', C. Moore, dir., *Elementary* series 1, episode 13 (CBS, New York, 2013).

Elementary, Robert Doherty, creator, CBS, New York, 2012 -.

'A Giant Gun, Filled with Drugs', Guy Ferland, dir., *Elementary* (CBS, New York, 2013).

Twilight [DVD], Catherine Hardwicke, dir. (Contender Entertainment Group, 2008)

Sherlock: Complete Series 1 & 2 [DVD], T. Haynes, Euros Lyn and Paul McGuigan, dirs. (BBC/2 Entertain, 2012)

Sherlock Holmes: A Game of Shadows [DVD], Guy Ritchie, dir. (Warner Bros, 2012)

The Dark Knight [DVD], Christopher Nolan, dir. (Warner Bros, 2009).

Star Wars Trilogy [DVD], George Lucas, dir. (Twentieth Century Fox, 2004 [1977–83]).

Online
'Final Boss'. *TV Tropes* [n.d.], http://tvtropes.org/pmwiki/pmwiki.php/Main/FinalBoss.

'YOU SEE, BUT YOU DO NOT OBSERVE. THE DISTINCTION IS CLEAR.'

SHERLOCK HOLMES
'A SCANDAL IN BOHEMIA'

Contributor Details

EDITORS

Tom Ue is Social Sciences and Humanities Research Council of Canada Doctoral Fellow and Canadian Centennial Scholar in the Department of English Language and Literature at University College London, where he researches Shakespeare's influence on the writing of Henry James, George Gissing and Oscar Wilde. Ue has taught at University College London. He was Visiting Scholar in the Department of English at Yale University, and the 2011 Cameron Hollyer Memorial Lecturer, and he has held an Everett Helm Visiting Fellowship. Although he specializes in nineteenth-century literature, he cares deeply about, and writes on, many aspects of intellectual history. He has published widely on Sherlock Holmes, and he is concurrently at work on a shorter piece on photography and phonography and their impact on the forms of late-Victorian and Edwardian writing. This is an opportunity to do some preliminary work towards a monograph on legal theory and the British novel in the nineteenth century.

Jonathan Cranfield is Lecturer in English Literature and Cultural History at Liverpool John Moores University. His research interests include Arthur Conan Doyle, Victorian periodicals, and relationships between literature and science. He has published various articles in these fields and is currently completing a monograph on the later fiction of Arthur Conan Doyle.

CONTRIBUTORS

Jonathan Barnes was born in 1979 and was educated in Norfolk and at Oxford University. He is the author of two novels, *The Somnambulist* (Gollancz, 2008) and *The Domino Men* (Gollancz, 2007)., as well as a number of Holmesian dramas. He contributes regularly to the *Times Literary Supplement* and to the *Literary Review*. He is now a Lecturer in Creative Writing at Kingston University.

Scott Beatty has been writing comic books and books about comic books since the last millennium (1999 to be precise), and is proud to say that he has chronicled a few of the adventures of fiction's greatest heroes, including (but not limited to) Batman, Buck Rogers, The Phantom, and most recently Sherlock Holmes.

Noel Brown received his Ph.D. in Film from Newcastle University in 2010, where he has taught courses on film and literature. Currently an independent scholar, his primary research interests are classical and modern Hollywood cinema, particularly the historical dimensions of the family film; children's film and television globally; contemporary youth cultures; and film genre. He is the author of The Hollywood Family Film: A History, from Shirley Temple to Harry Potter (I.B. Tauris, 2012), and the co-editor (with Bruce Babington) of the edited collection Beyond Disney: Children's Films and Family Films in Global Cinema (I.B. Tauris, forthcoming). He has written for several peer-reviewed journals, including The Historical Journal of Film, Radio and Television, *The Quarterly Review of Film and Video* and Scope: An Online Journal of Film and Television Studies, and has contributed to several books and other publications. He is currently researching the history of British children's cinema.

Huw-J Davies is a graduate of the Kubert school and holds a Ph.D. in Mythology from UCLA. An industry veteran who has worked tirelessly behind the scenes in both print and film media for over 27 years, he has racked up an impressive roll call for employers including Film Roman, Warner Bros., Disney, Weinstein, Fox, Marvel and Viacom.
Huw-J heads Hayena Studios along with Pummie-Productions, works on mixed-media projects such as directing Alice Cooper in a holographic show, FIFA and Coca Cola; is the creator of the Turds/Joe Turd's Turd World Brand; and is publishing books under the Pummie-Productions label including *Garth/Captain Garth Freeman of the Armed Services*, *Underpants Day* and *Tally Ho!* He is currently developing two animated series for the US TV networks and writing the second Young Sherlock Homes Adventures.

Anthony Horowitz is a TV screenwriter. He is the creator and writer of *Foyle's War*, *Midsomer Murders* and *Collision*, as well as the adaptor of many of Agatha Christie's Hercule Poirot novels for the ITV series. He was awarded a BAFTA for *Foyle's War* and Foyle was voted 'The People's Detective' in the ITV3 Crime Thriller Awards 2010, an award voted for by viewers. His new five-part drama series *Injustice* was shown on ITV1 in May. Anthony Horowitz is also the author of a string of bestselling children's books, including the Alex Rider series, which has sold 13 million copies worldwide, and *The Power of Five* and *The Diamond Brother* series. He lives in Clerkenwell, London.

Owen Jollands graduated from the University of Warwick with an MA in Physics and has had many jobs across many industries. Finding a creative outlet with Huw-J's Masterclass and graduating from the first intake, Owen went on to work on other projects for Markosia, Image and Zenescope comics and is currently working regularly for both Medikidz in the United Kingdom and HiFi Color Studios in the US.

Russell Merritt [*The Trepoff Murder*, 1960], when not reading Sherlock Holmes, teaches as a Visiting Professor in the Film Studies program at the University of California, Berkeley. He has written two books with J. B. Kaufman on Walt Disney's early films and has authored numerous articles on D. W. Griffith, Sergei Eisenstein, Disney, colour theory, animation, and early film. Professor Merritt also produced and directed the 'Great Nickelodeon Show', a recreation of a turn-of-the-century Nickelodeon program which has played at the Telluride Film Festival, Il Giornate del Cinema Muto, the Los Angeles Film Festival, and other venues.

Growing up in a small town in Indiana, USA, **Luke Benjamen Kuhns**'s passion for Sherlock Holmes began as a kid when he picked up *The Adventures of Sherlock Holmes* at the local library. The detective has, in some ways, always had an influence on him and, in 2012, he wrote the first of his *Untold Adventures* series: *The Untold Adventures of Sherlock Holmes* (MX Publishing here and subsequently). In 2013, he released volume 2: *Studies In Legacy*. He has written two Sherlock Holmes graphic novels: *Case of the Crystal Blue Bottle* (2012) and *The Horror of Frankenstein* (2013), as well as contributed to *Sherlock's Home: The Empty House* (2012) and *The Art of Deduction* (2013). He has also presented Holmes papers at The Great Sherlock Holmes Debates 2 and 3 and is an advocate for the Save Undershaw campaign.

Shane Peacock was born in 1957 in Thunder Bay, Ontario, one of four brothers. He attended school in the northern town of Kapuskasing, before attending university, where he studied history and English literature. A biographer, journalist and screenwriter, he is also the author of six novels and three plays, and has been nominated for numerous awards including several National Magazine Awards and the Arthur Ellis Award for crime fiction. When not writing, Shane Peacock enjoys playing hockey with his three children, and watching sumo wrestling. He lives near Cobourg, Ontario.

Shane Peacock is an author, playwright, documentary screenwriter and journalist, who writes for young readers and adults. He lives in a Victorian house in a protected forest about an hour northeast of Toronto, Ontario, Canada, with his family. The Boy Sherlock Holmes series has won and been nominated for more than fifty awards in Canada and the United States, and has so far been published in twelve languages in ten countries. He is also the author of *Last Message* (2012), one of the novels in the groundbreaking, 'Seven, The Series' project from Orca Books. A dynamic speaker, he frequently appears at conventions, writers' festivals, schools and universities, spreading the word not just about his work but concerning literacy and its importance to young people.

Shane is now working on a new series for young readers, a trilogy of horror/adventure novels set in late Victorian England and Scotland, influenced by the work of Edgar Allan Poe. A sequel to *Last Message*, this one influenced by Ian Fleming, Graham Greene, Roald Dahl and Daniel Craig, is also in the works.

Benjamin Poore is Lecturer in Theatre at the University of York. His first monograph, *Heritage, Nostalgia and Modern British Theatre* (Palgrave, 2012) was a history of stage representations of the Victorians since 1968. He has published articles and book chapters on stage and screen adaptations of Sherlock Holmes, Sweeney Todd, Sikes and Nancy, Queen Victoria and Dracula, and is currently planning an edited collection on neo-Victorian villains, and a second monograph on theatre and empire.

Robert Ryan was born in Liverpool and moved south to attend university. He graduated from Brunel with a MSc in Environmental Pollution Science, intending to go into teaching. Instead, he spent two years as a mechanic for a Hot Rod team, racing highly tuned Fords ('the fag-end of motorsport,' as Bernie Ecclestone called it). Eventually he did lecture, but at the same time freelanced for Nick Logan's *The Face* Magazine, *GQ*, *The Guardian*, *Sunday Times*, *Telegraph* and *Arena*. He subsequently took a position on staff at the *Sunday Times* as Deputy Travel Editor. It was while on assignment in Seattle that he came across the setting for his first novel, *Underdogs* (Headline Review, 2005). As well as continuing with journalism and novels, he regularly collaborates with jazz trumpeter and composer Guy Barker on various musical projects. His fifteenth book, *Dead Man's Land* (Simon & Schuster, 2013) imagines the career of Dr John Watson in World War I.

Born to British and Nigerian parents, most of **JL Straw**'s formative years were spent in Nigeria. She has been drawing all her life and has always had an interest in art and design. Computer games and two brothers were the biggest influence on her creativity and after sixteen years in Nigeria she came back to the United Kingdom in December 2006 and decided comics was the career for her. In 2008 she joined Huw-J's comic art Masterclass and continued on to work on The Young Sherlock Holmes Adventures. JL Straw now specializes in inking but continues to penciling and is currently working on her second graphic novel.

Ellie Ann Soderstrom was born in the jungles of Thailand, raised in a small farming village in Iowa, lived in the middle of a Texan desert, and now abides in the Ozarks. She is the Director of Publishing for Noble Beast, LLC, an enhanced book publisher. She authored *The Silver Sickle*, a young-adult science fiction, co-authored the Sarah Steele thriller series with Aaron Patterson, and wrote the multimedia adventure, *Slice of Life*, soon to be released. She writes enhanced comics for Motionworks Entertainment. She really likes connecting with people, especially those with geeky tendencies. You can find her on Twitter @*elliesoderstrom*; Facebook, Ellie Ann Author; or on her website, http://ellieann.net.

Image Credits

Additional Images

Inset:	© Public Domain
Chapter 2:	Fig. 1, p. 29 © Russell Merritt
	Fig. 2, p. 30 © KTTV
	Fig. 3, p. 32 © Chicago Tribune
	Fig. 4-5, pp. 33-34 © Realart
	Fig. 6, p. 35 © MPTV
	Fig. 7, p. 35 © MPTV

Fan Appreciation No. 2: All images (pp. 62 and 64) © Noble Beast

Chapter 4:	Fig. 1, p. 70 © Jonathan Cranfield
	Fig. 2, p. 74 © Public Domain
	Fig. 3, p. 74 © Public Domain

Fan Appreciation No. 3 All images (pp. 80, 83, and 85) © Markosia

Chapter 5:   All images (pp. 91, 93, 95, and 97) © DiC Entertainment / The Cookie Jar Company

Fan Appreciation No. 4: All images (pp. 100, 103, and 105) © Dynamite Entertainment

Chapter 6:   All images (pp. 111 and 115) © Big Finish

Chapter 7:   All images (pp. 119, 121, and 122) © Shane Peacock

Fan Appreciation No. 5:	Fig. 1, p. 126 © Simon & Schuster UK
	Fig. 2, p. 128 © BBC
	Fig. 3-4, pp. 130-31 © Ruby Cock- burn, British Red Cross Society
Chapter 8:	Fig. 1, p. 136 © Benjamin Poore
	Fig. 2, p. 139 © Public Domain
	Fig. 3-4, p. 140 © BBC
	Fig. 5, p. 141 © BBC
	Fig. 6, p. 141 © Warner Bros. / Village Roadshow Pictures / Silver Pictures
Inset:	p. 155 © Public Domain

'THE WORLD IS FULL OF OBVIOUS THINGS WHICH NOBODY BY ANY CHANCE EVER OBSERVES.'

SHERLOCK HOLMES
'THE HOUND OF THE BASKERVILLES'

FAN PHEN☆MENA

OTHER TITLES AVAILABLE IN THE SERIES

Star Trek
Edited by Bruce E. Drushel
ISBN: 978-1-78320-023-8
£15.50 / $22

Star Wars
Edited by Mika Elovaara
ISBN: 978-1-78320-022-1
£15.50 / $22

The Big Lebowski
Edited by Zachary Ingle
ISBN: 978-1-78320-202-7
£15.50 / $22

The Big Lebowski
Edited by Lynn Zubernis
and Katherine Larsen
ISBN: 978-1-78320-203-4
£15.50 / $22

Doctor Who
Edited by Paul Booth
ISBN: 978-1-78320-020-7
£15.50 / $22

Buffy the Vampire Slayer
Edited by Jennifer K. Stuller
ISBN: 978-1-78320-019-1
£15.50 / $22

Twin Peaks
Edited by Marisa C. Hayes
and Franck Boulegue
ISBN: 978-1-78320-024-5
£15.50 / $22

Audrey Hepburn
Edited by Jacqui Miller
ISBN: 978-1-78320-206-5
£15.50 / $22

For further information about the series
and news of forthcoming titles visit **www.intellectbooks.com**